Euthanasia

Look for these and other books in the Lucent Overview Series:

Abortion
Acid Rain
Adoption
Advertising
Alcoholism
Animal Rights
Artificial Organs
The Beginning of Writing
The Brain
Cancer
Censorship
Child Abuse
Children's Rights
Cities
The Collapse of the Soviet Union
Cults
Dealing with Death
Death Penalty
Democracy
Drug Abuse
Drugs and Sports
Drug Trafficking
Eating Disorders
Elections
Endangered Species
The End of Apartheid in South Africa
Energy Alternatives
Espionage
Ethnic Violence
Euthanasia
Extraterrestrial Life
Family Violence
Gangs
Garbage
Gay Rights
Genetic Engineering
The Greenhouse Effect
Gun Control
Hate Groups
Hazardous Waste
The Holocaust

Homeless Children
Homelessness
Illegal Immigration
Illiteracy
Immigration
Juvenile Crime
Memory
Mental Illness
Militias
Money
Ocean Pollution
Oil Spills
The Olympic Games
Organ Transplants
Ozone
The Palestinian-Israeli Accord
Pesticides
Police Brutality
Population
Poverty
Prisons
Rainforests
The Rebuilding of Bosnia
Recycling
The Reunification of Germany
Schools
Smoking
Space Exploration
Special Effects in the Movies
Sports in America
Suicide
The UFO Challenge
The United Nations
The U.S. Congress
The U.S. Presidency
Vanishing Wetlands
Vietnam
Women's Rights
World Hunger
Zoos

Euthanasia

by Lisa Yount

Lucent
Books

In memory of
JOE SUGUYAN
The beat goes on, but we miss yours.

Library of Congress Cataloging-in-Publication Data

Euthanasia / by Lisa Yount.
  p. cm. — (Lucent overview series)
Includes bibliographical references and index.
Summary: Discusses all forms of assisted death, including physician-assisted suicide, and the medical, legal, and ethical controversies surrounding euthanasia.
  ISBN 1-56006-697-0 (hardcover)
  1. Euthanasia—Juvenile literature.   [1. Euthanasia.
  2. Assisted suicide.] I. Title.   II. Series.
R726. Y67 2001
179.7—dc21   00-008065

Contents

INTRODUCTION   6

CHAPTER ONE   10
Changing Attitudes

CHAPTER TWO   25
Doctors and Death

CHAPTER THREE   40
Euthanasia and the Law

CHAPTER FOUR   55
Experiments in Euthanasia

CHAPTER FIVE   68
A Duty to Die?

NOTES   78
GLOSSARY   83
ORGANIZATIONS TO CONTACT   89
SUGGESTIONS FOR FURTHER READING   98
WORKS CONSULTED   102
INDEX   106
PICTURE CREDITS   112
ABOUT THE AUTHOR   112

Introduction

EUTHANASIA COMES FROM two Greek words meaning "good death." When English scholar and statesman Sir Francis Bacon coined the term in the early seventeenth century, he used it to mean the sort of "fair and easy passage from life"[1] that people hoped to have. A good death, of course, can mean different things to different people, just as a good life can. In present times as well as in Bacon's day, however, most people would probably say that it means dying peacefully and without pain, at home or in other pleasant surroundings, surrounded by loving family and friends.

The search for a "good death"

Today, growing numbers of people are unable to achieve this classic "good death." Advances in medical science, which added nearly thirty years to the average life expectancy in the United States during the twentieth century, have also prolonged the process of dying. High-tech medical machinery often confines dying people to the sterile, impersonal environment of a hospital, cutting them off from their homes and families.

In the last few decades, some people have come to feel that achieving a good death in modern times may require turning off the machinery of dying. When natural death is preceded by torturous pain or growing helplessness, they say, it may even mean taking steps to speed death's arrival. *Euthanasia* is the word that some use to refer to such hastening of death. In the broader of its modern meanings, *euthanasia* refers to any action that hastens the death of a terminally or incurably ill person. (A person is usually considered to be terminally ill when doctors expect him or her to survive for less than six months.) This action may be taken by doctors, family members, or the sick or dying people themselves.

Euthanasia can also have a more narrow or specific meaning: ending another person's life in order to stop the person's pain or suffering. This action has been popularly called mercy killing. *Euthanasia* in its narrower meaning does not include physician-assisted suicide, in which a sick person performs the action that causes death but requires the help of a doctor to carry it out. (Usually, the person

English scholar and statesman Sir Francis Bacon coined the term euthanasia *in the early seventeenth century.*

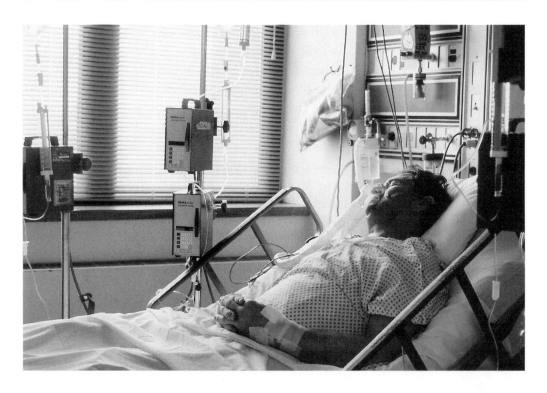

An intensive care patient breathes by means of a respirator, one of the many technological advances that prolong the dying process.

swallows lethal medication prescribed for the purpose by a physician.) The broader meaning of *euthanasia*, however, does cover physician-assisted suicide as well as other forms of assisted death. In the 1990s much of the debate about euthanasia (in its broader meaning) focused on physician-assisted suicide. This book's title uses *euthanasia* in its wider sense, refering to all forms of assisted death, including physician-assisted suicide. In the text, however, *euthanasia* is usually used in its narrower meaning of death caused by another person.

Conflicting values

Medicine and law influence people's feelings and decisions about physician-assisted suicide and euthanasia, but deciding whether these actions are right or wrong is a matter of ethics. Like all difficult ethical questions, this one represents a conflict among several values that most people regard highly. Each person must decide which of these values means the most to him or her. "Ethical dilemmas arise not when we want to do something evil but when we want to do something good," ethicist David Heim writes in *Christian Century*. "The dilemmas arise because the good we want to accomplish conflicts with some other good we also want to accomplish or preserve."[2] The conflict, then, is not between good and evil, but between two courses of action that may seem equally good.

To many people, especially those with certain religious backgrounds, preserving life is the greatest good. They believe that the Sixth Commandment in the Old Testament of the Bible says it all: "Thou shalt not kill." They believe the commandment applies to killing oneself or to killing someone else who has asked to die, even a terminally ill person in great pain, just as much as to any other form of killing. Other people feel that the greatest value is autonomy—independence and self-determination, the right to control one's own life and death. Some people want above all to relieve suffering, even when the only possible relief is death. Still others say that the risk that vulnerable people, such as the sick or disabled, might be persuaded or even forced to die is more important than the suffering of a few.

The morality of all forms of assisted death—euthanasia in its broader meaning—was hotly debated in the last decades of the twentieth century, and the debate is sure to continue and perhaps even intensify in the twenty-first century. This subject arouses such strong feelings because it involves people's most deeply cherished beliefs. As federal appeals court judge Stephen Reinhardt wrote in 1996, the issue of assisted death

> requires us to confront the most basic of human concerns—the mortality of self and loved ones—and to balance the interest in preserving human life against the desire to die peacefully and with dignity. . . . [This] controversy . . . may touch more people more profoundly than any other issue the courts will face in the foreseeable future.[3]

1

Changing Attitudes

THE MOVEMENT TO make assisted death legal has often been called the right-to-die movement. The term may seem more than a little strange at first. Death, after all, is guaranteed to everyone, although most people try to avoid it as long as they can. Who, then, could possibly need, let alone want, a "right" to die?

Of course, the movement's members say, what they want is not really a right to die. Rather, they ask for the right to have some control over the time and manner of their death. Barbara Dority, a leader in the Washington State branch of the Hemlock Society, a major right-to-die organization, says that "the right to die with dignity, in our own time and on our own terms," is the "ultimate civil right."[4]

First discussions of euthanasia

Until the late twentieth century, few people would have dreamed of demanding a right to die. Death came all too soon to most, and doctors could do little to stop it. Many people died of infectious diseases such as pneumonia, which killed quickly.

Not all deaths were quick or easy, of course. Cancer, for instance, has existed since the beginning of humankind, and it can bring a slow and painful death. From time to time throughout history, doctors or family members no doubt gave people with painful, incurable illnesses an overdose of medicine or in some other way helped them die a little sooner than nature would have allowed. Alternatively, some helped the incurably ill kill themselves. Most religions considered such actions immoral, however. They were almost universally illegal as well, so they had to be carried out in strict secrecy.

Only in the late nineteenth and early twentieth centuries did a few doctors and others begin to discuss these practices openly and to refer to them as euthanasia. A group called the Voluntary Euthanasia Society formed in Britain in 1935, for example, and a similar group, the Euthanasia Society of America, was created in 1938. Such groups urged that laws be changed to permit euthanasia, usually at the hands of a doctor, if a sick person requested it. A few famous people joined these groups—the British organization boasted novelist H. G. Wells, playwright George Bernard Shaw, and philosopher Bertrand Russell among its members, for instance—and polls showed that about half the public supported at least some of their aims. Nonetheless, their efforts to legalize euthanasia always failed.

H. G. Wells was a member of a British organization that urged lawmakers to permit euthanasia if a patient requested it.

The Nazi "euthanasia" program

Public support for euthanasia reached a low point just after World War II, when people around the world learned about a secret program that Germany's Nazi (National Socialist) government had carried out between 1939 and 1941. Beginning with children and then moving on to adults, the Nazi "euthanasia" program eventually murdered some one hundred thousand mentally or physically disabled Germans whom the government considered to be unworthy of life.

The Nazis did not ask the disabled people or their family members whether they wanted to die. Instead, they transported the people to distant places, killed them in gas chambers, and then burned their bodies. The Nazis went on to do the same thing to six million Jews and others whom they considered undesirable. The euthanasia program, in fact,

The Nazis used crematoriums to burn the bodies of Jews and others whom they considered undesirable.

proved to be a kind of dress rehearsal for the Holocaust's later executions.

The Nazi program gave the idea of euthanasia a horror-story air that some people feel it has never escaped. Changes in medicine and society during the 1950s and 1960s, however, made others begin thinking once more that euthanasia, or at least some form of assisted dying, might not always be wrong.

Prolonging the dying process

Starting in the 1940s, advances in medical science helped more people in industrialized countries live into old age. A combination of better living conditions and antibiotics such as penicillin brought many infectious diseases under control. Growing numbers of people therefore survived long enough to die of illnesses that most often struck the old, such as heart disease, cancer, and Alzheimer's disease. Death from these diseases often came only after years of slow and sometimes painful loss of physical or mental abilities.

In hospitals, inventions such as feeding tubes and respirators allowed doctors to hold off death for people who could no longer eat, drink, or breathe on their own. Such devices seemed like miracles when they rescued people who eventually returned to health or could at least enjoy life. When they merely put off an inevitable end for those in incurable pain or who were permanently unconscious, however, some people began to see them instead as tools of torture.

These inventions also changed the surroundings in which many deaths occur. Traditionally, before these medical advances, most people had died at home. As use of elaborate medical technology to prolong life became more common, however, more and more dying people were brought to hospitals, where the technology was available. By 1978, 71 percent of U.S. citizens died in hospitals, and the figure had risen to more than 80 percent in the late 1990s.

These high-tech hospital deaths all too often were anything but a "fair and easy passage from life." In the 1994 book *How We Die*, physician and science writer Sherwin Nuland describes the typical modern death scene as filled with

> beeping and squealing monitors, the hissing of respirators and pistoned mattresses, the flashing multicolored electronic signals—the whole technological panoply [that] is background for the tactics by which we are deprived of the tranquillity we have every right to hope for, and separated from those few who would not let us die alone.[5]

The "rights culture"

At the same time that medical advances were changing the nature of dying, other events changed the way people viewed their rights in general, including the right to make decisions about death. In the civil rights movement of the early 1960s, African Americans demanded an end to laws and customs that treated them as inferiors. The women's rights movement followed in the early 1970s. In short, a wide variety of people began insisting that they had a basic

During the last forty years, many people (like these students at Columbia University) have demanded the right to control their own lives.

right to control their lives. Many specific rights, such as the right to be protected against discrimination, came to be guaranteed by law.

In this "rights culture," people soon began to change the way they made health care decisions. A decade or two earlier, at the height of medicine's midcentury advances, most patients had admired their doctors and left medical decisions entirely to them. By the 1970s, however, many people no longer had close, friendly relationships with their physicians. They saw the medical profession as cold and greedy, more interested in making money than in looking out for its patients. The result was the patients' rights movement. People demanded a greater role in making choices about their health care, including the right to refuse treatment, even if that treatment were necessary to sustain their lives.

Attitudes toward death were also changing at this time. During the earlier part of the century, most people had avoided discussing or even mentioning death whenever possible. Around the beginning of the 1970s, however, death moved rather suddenly from a taboo subject to almost an obsession. *On Death and Dying*, a book by Swiss-born psychiatrist Elisabeth Kübler-Ross, was one of the first to bring the topic into the open. "No other single person has so dramatically turned around a whole generation of opinion-makers on a single subject,"[6] one reporter wrote of her. Published in 1969, *On Death and Dying* became a best-seller, and a host of similar books and articles soon followed. "Death is now selling books,"[7] the editors of *Publishers Weekly* noted in 1974.

Karen Quinlan's tragedy

All of these factors—medical technology that was seemingly out of control, the rise of the rights culture, patients' demands for a greater say in health care decisions, and an increased willingness to talk about death—came together in Americans' reactions to a tragic court case that made headlines in 1976. It began on April 14, 1975, when a twenty-one-year-old New Jersey woman named Karen Ann Quinlan went to a party, consumed a mixture of drugs and

Karen Ann Quinlan slipped into a coma after consuming a mixture of drugs and alcohol at a party.

alcohol, and became unconscious. When friends noticed that her breathing had stopped, she was rushed to a hospital. Doctors there were unable to restart her natural breathing, so they connected her to a respirator. The respirator kept her alive, but she did not regain consciousness.

Karen's parents, Joseph and Julia Quinlan, spent agonized months by her bedside, watching her weight drop from 115 to 90 pounds and her contracting muscles slowly draw her body into a twisted posture. Robert Morse, the physician assigned to Karen, informed her parents that she was in a persistent vegetative state (PVS), popularly called a coma. She had cycles of sleeping and waking, but she was not really aware of her environment. In all likelihood, Karen's parents were told, she would never regain full consciousness because the higher centers of her brain had been damaged beyond repair. Only her brain stem, which controls the body's automatic responses, remained active.

At the end of July 1975 the Quinlans, after much painful thought, decided that only the respirator was keeping Karen from an unavoidable natural death. They asked St. Clare's, the hospital where she was being cared for, to turn it off. Morse and the hospital administration refused, saying that doing so was against their medical ethics. ("You have to understand our position," Sister Urban, the head of the St. Clare's board of trustees, later told Julia Quinlan. "In this hospital we don't kill people."[8]) The Quinlans then went to court, asking that Joseph Quinlan be made Karen's legal guardian so he would have the right to insist that the hospital turn off the respirator.

Robert Muir Jr., the first judge who heard the case, ruled against the Quinlans on November 10. Letting Joseph Quinlan be Karen's guardian would not be in her best interest, he said. Muir agreed that Karen would have had the right to refuse treatment, even life-sustaining treatment, if she had been competent upon her admission to the hospital. Since she was not, however, Muir felt that the government must take on the duty of preserving her life. "There is no constitutional right to die that can be asserted by a parent for his incompetent adult child,"[9] he ruled. Julia Quinlan had testified that, when speaking of two acquaintances' slow deaths from cancer, Karen had said that she would not want to be kept alive like that, but Muir said that Karen had made only a theoretical statement, not a direct decision about her own health care.

The Quinlans appealed the case, and the New Jersey Supreme Court heard it in January 1976. Reversing the lower court, the New Jersey justices ruled on March 31 that, given Karen's incurable unconsciousness, her apparent wishes not to remain alive outweighed the state's normally powerful interest in preserving life.

Ironically, this seeming victory did not end the Quinlans' tragedy. By the time Julia and Joseph Quinlan

transferred Karen to a nursing home that was willing to turn off her respirator, she had become able to breathe on her own, though her condition was not improved in any other way. She lingered on in her twilight world for another decade, finally dying of pneumonia on June 13, 1986.

Julia Quinlan (right) attends a news conference to announce the formation of a coalition to create more compassionate care for the terminally ill.

A boost for advance directives

The Quinlan case generated a huge amount of publicity—and fear. People began looking for ways to keep something like the Quinlans' disaster from happening to them or their loved ones. One possibility that many discovered was the living will, a document that stated what medical treatments should be accepted or refused on a person's behalf if he or she became unable to make health care decisions. Living wills had existed since 1969 but had received little attention. More importantly, they had no legal force. Hospitals and doctors tended to ignore them even in the rare cases in which patients had filled them out. A few states had introduced legislation to make living wills legally binding, but no such laws had ever been passed.

The Quinlan story, however, brought new media coverage of living wills and a huge upsurge in public demand for these documents. Between 1969 and 1975, for example, the Euthanasia Education Council, which promoted and distributed living wills, sent out 750,000 blank copies of the document. During the following year and a half, it mailed out 1.25 million copies.

The fight to give legal power to living wills also began to succeed. Barry Keene, a California legislator who had introduced an unsuccessful state bill to give these health care documents legal standing in 1974, reintroduced the bill in 1976, and this time it passed. Keene pinpointed the most likely reason for the change when he said, "The image of Karen Quinlan haunts our dreams."[10] Keene's bill, the Natural Death Act, became the first state law to recognize living wills. In the following decade, thirty-six other states made similar laws.

Interest in living wills continued to grow during the 1980s, sparking interest in other advance directives as well. The durable power of attorney for health care, or health care proxy, was another advance directive that became popular during this time. Rather than specifying particular medical treatments, this document names an individual to make health care decisions on behalf of the signer if the signer becomes unable to do so. An influential 1983 report by the President's Commission for the Study of Ethical Problems in Medicine and Biomedical and Behavioral Research recommended this form of advance directive. The durable power of attorney had legal force in all fifty states by 1986.

The Cruzan case

Meanwhile, court cases, some of them widely publicized, slowly broadened the debate about what kinds of life-sustaining treatments could be refused. Most people had no trouble thinking of a respirator as a medical treatment, but the issue became cloudier when the "treatments" were food and water, even if they were delivered through a tube. Joseph and Julia Quinlan, for example, never considered cutting off Karen's food and water. "That would be like killing Karen, and we couldn't live with that,"[11] Julia Quinlan once said.

Food and water were an issue in the first euthanasia case to reach the U.S. Supreme Court, a case that asked whether or not someone had the right to refuse life-sustaining medical treatment for someone else. Like the Quinlan case, it involved a young woman in a permanent coma and her grieving parents. The woman in this case was Nancy Beth Cruzan, whose brain had been damaged when her car skidded out of control on an icy Missouri road in 1983. Unlike Karen Quinlan, Cruzan could breathe on her own from the beginning, but doctors agreed that her chances of regaining consciousness were just as slim as Quinlan's had been.

After four years of waiting for a miracle that did not happen, Nancy's parents, Joe and Joyce Cruzan, asked the nursing home caring for her to remove the tube that carried

Nurses monitor an intensive care patient.

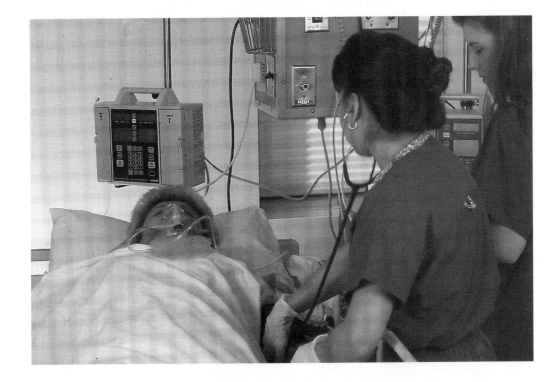

nutrition into her stomach. As had happened with the Quinlans, the institution refused, and the parents went to court. The chief issue in this case was what Nancy herself would have wanted. Although a housemate reported a somewhat serious conversation with her in which she had said that she would not want to be kept alive if she could not "live halfway normally,"[12] Nancy had not left an advance directive or even any very precise spoken statements about her wishes. Reversing a lower court that had supported the Cruzans, the Missouri Supreme Court ruled in November 1988 that the parents could not have the feeding tube removed because Nancy had not left clear and convincing evidence of her feelings about refusing medical treatment.

The Cruzans made a final appeal to the Supreme Court, which agreed to hear the case. The justices made their ruling on June 25, 1990. The Cruzan case was important, Chief Justice William Rehnquist wrote in the Court's majority opinion, because it was "the first case in which we have been squarely presented with the issue of whether the United States Constitution grants what is in common parlance [speech] referred to as a right to die."[13]

Chief Justice William Rehnquist.

The majority of the Supreme Court justices, like those of the New Jersey Supreme Court in the Quinlan case, agreed that Nancy Cruzan would have had the right to refuse life-sustaining treatment, including food and water, if she had been competent to make her own decisions. Indeed, Rehnquist wrote, the Court's previous decisions supported the assumption that the Constitution itself protected this right. Nonetheless, he went on, "there can be no [denying the government's] interest in the protection and preservation of human life."[14] Therefore, Missouri's demand for clear and convincing evidence of Cruzan's wishes was also constitutional because it was a sensible way of carrying out that duty.

The Supreme Court upheld the Missouri court's ruling against the Cruzans. Additional testimony from some of Nancy's friends, however, later convinced the Missouri court of her wishes, and the Cruzans were ultimately allowed to remove the feeding tube. Nancy Cruzan died on December 26, 1990, a little less than two weeks after the tube was removed.

With the Supreme Court's ruling on the Cruzan case, the notion that a competent, incurably ill adult has the right to refuse all forms of life-sustaining medical treatment was firmly fixed in law. Medical associations, most religious groups, and (according to polls) about three-fourths of the American public accepted this idea as well. Most people also agreed that surrogates, or substitute decision makers designated in such documents as durable powers of attorney, could ethically refuse treatment on behalf of formerly competent people who had left clear indications of their wishes. In other words, letting someone die, known as passive euthanasia, was acceptable.

A move toward active aid in dying

For some people, however, the right to be allowed to die was not enough. They believed that terminally ill people also had, or at least should have, the legal right to ask for more active help to end their suffering: assistance in suicide or, if a person were physically unable to commit suicide (could not lift or swallow pills, for example), death at another's hands.

One of the chief spokespeople for this view was Derek Humphry. A British-born journalist specializing in civil rights issues, Humphry first encountered the painful choices involved in hastening death in 1975 while he was still living in England. His wife, Jean, was in terrible pain from incurable cancer, and she asked him to help her commit suicide. After much discussion, Humphry agreed, even though he knew that such an action was against the law. He obtained a prescription for a lethal dose of medicine from a doctor whom he never named and, when Jean said she was ready, he gave it to her. In 1978 he published a book about the experience called *Jean's*

British-born journalist Derek Humphry and his second wife founded the Hemlock Society in 1980.

Way. British authorities then investigated Jean's death, but they decided not to prosecute Humphry.

Humphry moved to California, and in 1980 he and his second wife, Ann Wickett, founded a group they called the Hemlock Society. The name refers to the poison that the ancient Greek philosopher Socrates drank in 399 B.C. after the city-state of Athens convicted him of corrupting the city's young people with his teachings and ordered him to commit suicide. Socrates had died peacefully, discussing philosophy with his students to the last. The Hemlock Society's purpose, Humphry said, was to help modern people attain a similarly peaceful death by "promot[ing] a climate of public opinion which is tolerant of the right of people who are terminally ill to end their lives in a planned manner."[15] Ultimately, the Hemlock Society hoped to see physician-assisted suicide, or perhaps even euthanasia, made legal for terminally ill people.

Humphry's views caused considerable controversy, especially after he published a second book, *Let Me Die*

Before I Wake, in 1981. This book not only contained true stories of people who had helped suffering loved ones commit suicide but also included practical information about doing so, such as doses of common drugs that were likely to be fatal. Other right-to-die groups focused on promoting and distributing advance directives and informing people about their right to refuse medical treatment, not on suicide or active euthanasia. They were afraid that people who were unhappy but not terminally ill would misuse Humphry's information and that resulting public disapproval would damage their own cause. "I only hope the backlash [from your book] doesn't sink us all,"[16] Ann Jane Levinson, executive director of Concern for Dying (the new name of the Euthanasia Education Council), wrote to Humphry soon after *Let Me Die* was published.

Support for assisted death grows

Only a tiny minority of Americans shared Humphry's views during the early 1980s, but as the decade went on,

Socrates (seated) drinks hemlock after the city-state of Athens ordered him to commit suicide.

those views gained support from some members of another group that, although also small compared to the total population, was vocal and growing: people with AIDS. This disease, first identified in 1982, soon reached highly publicized epidemic proportions.

Because the AIDS virus destroys the immune system, people suffering from the disease die slow and often painful deaths from a variety of infections that their bodies cannot fight off. After seeing friends and lovers suffer this way, some people with the disease began saving lethal doses of medication to use if their own illnesses became too much to bear. They also began demanding the right to ask for such medication legally. As reporter Gary L. Thomas writes, "Instead of broken and weary 80-year-old citizens dealing with life-threatening diseases . . . , affluent 25- to 35-year-old men—eager and able to extend their political clout and organization—suddenly joined the debate"[17] on assisted suicide and euthanasia. These people gave the more radical wing of the right-to-die movement— the part that supported active assistance in suicide rather than simply letting die and honoring advance directives— a new burst of energy and urgency.

By the start of the 1990s, attitudes toward hastening a terminally ill person's death had changed considerably. "Taken as a whole," a 1999 review of opinion polls concluded, "the trend data [for the 1980s] show a growth of support for various consensual practices [actions taken with a patient's consent] that result in the death of terminally ill patients."[18] The practices people supported were beginning to include not only the termination of medical treatment but also active assistance in dying by the same professionals who had become so skilled at fighting off death: physicians.

2

Doctors and Death

I swear by Apollo [the Greek god of the sun and of medicine] . . . and all the gods and goddesses . . . that I will fulfill . . . this oath. . . . I will apply . . . measures for the benefit of the sick according to my ability and judgment; I will keep them from harm and injustice.[19]

DOCTORS OFTEN SPEAK these solemn words, part of a pledge called the Hippocratic oath, when they graduate from medical school. The oath is credited to a Greek physician named Hippocrates, who lived in the fourth century B.C. Even though it was written long ago, many physicians still *Ancient Greek* consider the Hippocratic oath a basic statement of the *physician Hippocrates.* medical profession's ethics and duties. Chief among these is "do no harm." The oath goes on to name one particular form of harm that a doctor must promise not to do: "I will neither give a deadly drug to anybody if asked for it, nor will I make a suggestion to that effect."[20]

But some people today are asking, What is harm? If a patient cannot be cured and is dying in torment, is giving a fatal prescription or injection at the person's request harming or helping? Should the command to "give no deadly drug" always be honored, or is it in some ways as old-fashioned as swearing by ancient gods?

"Dr. Death"

Doctors have always had to face the difficult dilemma of what to do about a suffering, dying patient, but that dilemma has never been more widely discussed than in the 1990s, when the decisions that some physicians made about assisted suicide and euthanasia produced headlines. These discussions have forced both doctors and patients to think hard about what a physician's duties are when healing becomes impossible.

Until recent years, most doctors had little doubt about what their duties were. They cured disease when they could, tried to improve patients' quality of life when they could not cure, and above all, preserved life for as long as possible. They were trained to see death as an enemy and losing a patient as a personal failure, even when the death occurred through no fault of their own. Once life-sustaining treatment such as attachment to a respirator was begun, many physicians, like Robert Morse in the Karen Quinlan case, felt that it should not be discontinued as long as any hope of life remained. The American Medical Association, the chief physicians' association in the United States, opposed disconnecting respirators or feeding tubes from patients in persistent vegetative states, even at the request of an advance directive or a surrogate, until 1986.

Just four years later, however, a retired Michigan pathologist named Jack Kevorkian startled the country by proposing a very different role for doctors. (Like other pathologists, Kevorkian had a medical degree, but his job had been examining dead bodies for signs of disease. He had never treated living patients.) If terminally or even incurably ill people asked to die, Kevorkian said, physicians like himself had a duty to help them do so. As he began explaining on television talk shows in 1989, he had built a machine that, when a patient triggered it, injected a substance to make the person unconscious and then, a few minutes later, a second drug to stop the heart. He called his device a Mercitron.

One person who heard Kevorkian's message was a fifty-four-year-old Oregon woman named Janet Adkins. Adkins

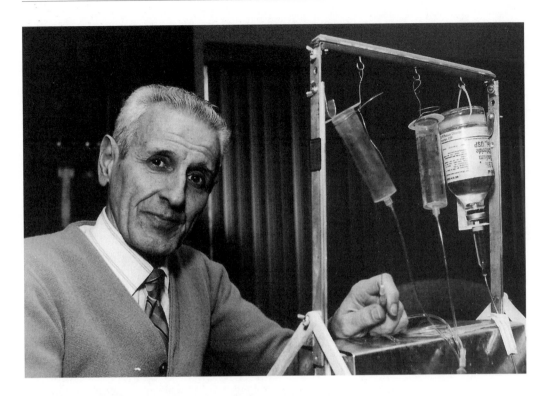

had just learned that she had Alzheimer's disease, an incurable illness that progressively destroys memory and brain function. As she wrote, "I don't choose to put my family or myself through the agony of this terrible disease."[21] She asked Kevorkian to help her end her life. On June 4, 1990, in the back of Kevorkian's battered van, Janet Adkins became the first person to die by the Mercitron.

She was far from the last. Kevorkian claims he helped some 150 people die during the 1990s. He could no longer obtain drugs for the Mercitron after Michigan's state medical board suspended his medical license in 1991, so for later assisted suicides he used a different apparatus through which people breathed odorless, deadly carbon monoxide gas.

Some people, including the families of many of those who came to him, have praised Kevorkian's actions. One family member called him "an angel."[22] Others viewed him with outrage, terming him "Dr. Death" or "Jack the Dripper."[23] The only thing everyone could agree on was

Dr. Kevorkian poses next to a machine he uses to perform physician-assisted suicide.

that, as journalist Sue Woodman writes in *Last Rights: The Struggle over the Right to Die*, "Kevorkian has single-handedly done more to highlight the issue of physician-assisted suicide than anyone else in the world."[24]

A controversial figure

Even many people who believed that the terminally ill should have the right to ask doctors to help them commit suicide disapproved of Jack Kevorkian. Part of the problem was Kevorkian's personality: He courted the media, bragged about his actions, and criticized the medical profession, whom he called "hypocritic oafs."[25] Rather than changing laws against assisted suicide and euthanasia, as most of the right-to-die movement wanted to do, he preferred to ignore or challenge such laws.

Criticism of Kevorkian went deeper than dislike of his attitude, though. Right-to-die groups complained about

A woman expresses her support for physician-assisted suicide in a demonstration outside the Supreme Court in Washington, D.C.

him because he ignored safeguards that most of them wanted to see built into laws allowing physician-assisted suicide. For example, many of the people he helped to die were not terminally ill, which most groups wanted to make a requirement for requesting help in dying. Derek Humphry wrote in 1992,

> By helping three people who were not in the usual sense "terminally ill," Dr. Kevorkian has widened the debate over the ethics and legality of the right to choose to die. I believe the widening to be regrettable because the Hemlock movement and its sister organizations are close to the point of success in law reform. . . . Now Dr. Kevorkian has muddied the waters.[26]

Worse still, although all of the people who came to Kevorkian believed they were incurably ill, autopsies on several of them found no sign of physical disease. Thus, they may have suffered only from depression or other psychological problems that could have been treated. Kevorkian made little attempt to verify their medical conditions or have other doctors do so. Kevorkian has also been criticized for not trying to change people's minds about dying, for instance by discussing pain relief or other treatments that might have made their lives more bearable.

Kevorkian was put on trial for murder or assisted suicide five times, but the first four trials resulted in one mistrial and three acquittals. The acquittals came partly because, unlike many other states, Michigan did not then have a clear, permanent law against assisted suicide. Jurors also responded to the emotional appeals that Kevorkian and his lawyer, Geoffrey Fieger, made as they provided evidence of the people's wish to die. "I don't feel it's our obligation to choose for someone else how much pain and suffering that they can go through,"[27] one juror said.

In September 1998, however, Kevorkian stepped farther over the legal line: He personally administered a fatal drug to a patient. A jury convicted him of murder for this act in March 1999. He was sentenced to ten to twenty-five years in prison—in effect a life sentence since he was seventy

A police officer stands guard as Dr. Kevorkian (bottom left) talks to his attorney.

years old at the time. Judge Jessica Cooper told him sternly at his sentencing,

> You had the audacity to go on national television [A tape showing Kevorkian giving the drug injection had been shown, with his permission, on the CBS news program *60 Minutes* in November 1998.], show the world what you did and dare the legal system to stop you. Well, sir, consider yourself stopped.[28]

A gentler advocate

Soon after Jack Kevorkian began drawing public attention to physician-assisted suicide, a second and less disturbing medical spokesperson for the practice appeared. He was Timothy Quill, an experienced physician on the staff of New York's University of Rochester School of Medicine and Genesee Hospital. In March 1991 Quill published an article in the prestigious *New England Journal of Medicine* in which he admitted writing a prescription for a woman, whom he identified only as "Diane," knowing that she would use the drugs to kill herself. Diane, who had been Quill's patient for eight years, was terminally ill with leukemia (blood cancer). "I wrote the prescription with an uneasy feeling about the boundaries I was exploring—spiritual, legal, professional and personal," Quill wrote. "Yet I also felt strongly that I was setting [Diane] free to get the most out of the time she had left, and to maintain dignity and control on her own terms until her death."[29]

Even after an anonymous person leaked Diane's last name to authorities and an autopsy confirmed that she had died of a drug overdose, a grand jury decided not to charge Quill with any crime. The reaction to his article nonetheless turned Quill into an active supporter of physician-assisted suicide, although, he says, he is a reluctant one. "I'm not really an advocate of assisted suicide," he claims. "I'm an advocate of not abandoning people."[30]

Quill believes that doctors should help their patients die only as a last resort, when all attempts to relieve pain and other problems have failed. Unlike Kevorkian, he maintains that physicians who assist in suicide should know their patients well. Also, along with most other supporters of physician-assisted suicide, he wants to see the practice protected by safeguards that might prevent the sort of mistakes that Kevorkian and some of his patients apparently made, such as a requirement for consultation with another physician or a psychiatrist before a suicide request is granted. "Quill presented the gentle, thoughtful face of compassionate medicine. . . . His philosophy seemed to be the one most likely to succeed in the long term in the United States,"[31] Derek Humphry and Mary Clement wrote in 1998.

Doctors' secret acts

Quill and Kevorkian were forcing open discussion of a situation that doctors have always faced and some have always acted on. The most common way of dealing with

Dr. Timothy Quill (center) confronts the media following the 1997 Vacco vs. Quill court case.

this situation is a practice called terminal sedation, or the double effect. In terminal sedation, a physician gives a terminally ill, suffering patient a high dose of narcotics for the purpose of relieving the person's pain, knowing that the drugs may also have a second effect of shortening or even perhaps ending the person's life. Howard Grossman of the St. Luke's–Roosevelt Hospital at Columbia University calls terminal sedation "the dirty little secret of medicine . . . the tremendous burden that physicians have carried with them for a long, long time, the fact that they already help people out [to die]."[32]

Terminal sedation is generally considered legal, and even groups that strongly disapprove of physician-assisted suicide or euthanasia, such as the Catholic Church and the American Medical Association, accept its use. They say that the difference between this practice and euthanasia is in the intention of the physician: In terminal sedation, the physician may foresee the patient's hastened death but does not specifically intend it.

Surveys have repeatedly shown that some physicians go further than terminal sedation, although few are as open about it as Kevorkian and Quill—which is understandable since assisted suicide and euthanasia are illegal almost everywhere. Of 355 cancer specialists in the United States who were interviewed in a 1998 survey, for example, 56 (15.8 percent) admitted having committed euthanasia or having written prescriptions to assist in suicide. (Some, however, may have included terminal sedation in these categories.)

Should physicians be allowed to kill?

It is not surprising that terminally or incurably ill people who are thinking about killing themselves or wishing to be killed should turn to physicians. Doctors have access to drugs that can bring death surely and painlessly. They know what doses to use and how to administer them. Physicians, patients, and the general public, however, have strongly disagreed about whether doctors should ever be legally permitted to end patients' lives deliberately.

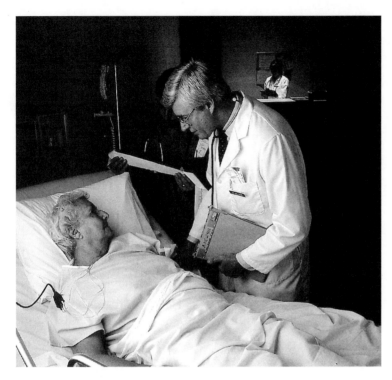

The question of whether or not doctors should legally be allowed to help patients die sparks heated debate among physicians, patients, and the general public.

Most major medical associations, including the American Medical Association (AMA) and the American Nurses Association, strongly oppose legalizing assisted suicide or euthanasia, even if it is done at the request of a terminally ill person. Thomas Reardon, chairman of the AMA Task Force on Quality Care at the End of Life, says that for a physician to intentionally cause the death of a patient "is fundamentally incompatible with the physician's role as healer and caregiver."[33] Supporters of legalization, however, say that people like Reardon take too narrow a view of a physician's duty. When healing is impossible, they believe, the doctor's job changes from healer to comforter. If all other methods of easing patients' pain and suffering fail, the best way to comfort them may be to help them end their lives or, if they cannot do so on their own, to do it for them. Else Borst-Eilers, the Netherlands' minister of health, has said, "There are situations in which the best way to heal the patient is to help him die peacefully, and the doctor who in such a situation grants the patient's request acts as the healer *par excellence*."[34]

Supporters of physician-assisted suicide also question the distinction between letting die and killing. Federal Second Circuit Court of Appeals judge Roger Miner wrote in an important 1996 right-to-die ruling, "Physicians do not fulfill the role of 'killer' by prescribing drugs to hasten death any more than they do by disconnecting life-support systems."[35] Marcia Angell, editor of the *New England Journal of Medicine*, adds, "We should ask ourselves not so much whether the doctor's role [in the death] is passive or active but whether the *patient's* role is passive or active."[36]

Finally, medical groups oppose legalization of assisted suicide and euthanasia because they believe that patients' trust in their doctors, a vital part of the medical relationship, would be seriously damaged if patients knew that their physicians had the legal right to kill them. Supporters of legalization claim, though, that allowing physicians to hasten death at patients' request might restore trust rather than destroy it. For instance, Angell writes, "I believe distrust is more likely to arise from uncertainty about whether a doctor will honor a patient's wishes"[37] than from the knowledge that the doctor would assist in suicide or euthanasia if the patient requested it.

Comforting the dying

Both supporters and opponents of physician-assisted suicide and euthanasia agree on one thing: Doctors need to take better care of people near the end of their lives. A 1999 survey indicated that 15 percent of patients dying from cancer and 23 percent of those dying from other illnesses had unmet needs for care. The AMA's Thomas Reardon has called the growing public support for physician-assisted suicide "a wake-up call, a message to our profession that we are not meeting our patients' needs."[38]

When a patient cannot be cured, the health care team's goal changes from restoring health and prolonging life to providing what is called palliative, or comfort, care. The

World Health Organization states that the purpose of palliative care is

> the achievement of the best possible quality of life for patients and their families. . . . Palliative care affirms life and regards dying as a normal process; neither hastens nor postpones death; provides relief from pain and other distressing symptoms; integrates the psychological and spiritual aspects of patient care; [and] offers a support system to help the family cope during the patient's illness and in their own bereavement.[39]

Health care institutions called hospices are devoted entirely to palliative care for the dying. British physician Dame Cicely Saunders founded St. Christopher's, the first modern hospice, in London in 1967. The first American hospice opened its doors in New Haven, Connecticut, in 1974. In the late 1990s there were about three thousand hospice programs in the United States. Hospice has become a philosophy as well as a type of institution, and hospice workers today help many people die comfortably

A social worker (far right) from the Visiting Nurses Association hospice program comforts a woman dying of cancer.

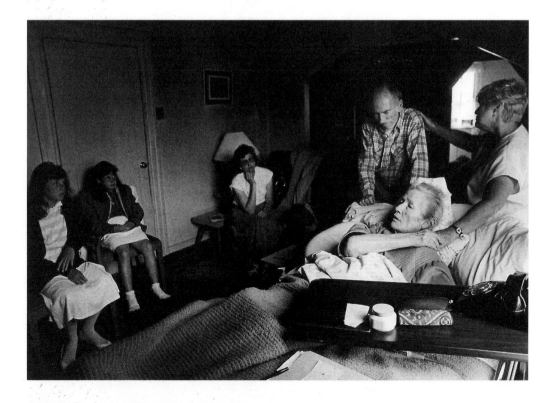

at home. Only about a fifth of Americans who died in 1997 received hospice care, however.

The AMA and many other groups and individual ethicists claim that if all dying people received the best hospice and palliative care, including thorough control of pain and treatment for the depression that frequently accompanies severe illness, most or all of the demand for physician-assisted suicide and euthanasia would vanish. Drug treatment and counseling for depression, which often goes unrecognized in sick or old people because doctors see it as a "normal" response to their condition, may be especially important. Ira Katz, director of geriatric psychiatry (psychiatry for elderly people) at the University of Pennsylvania School of Medicine, says,

> I truly believe that even in a nursing home, even in someone with heart failure, even with disabling arthritis, with Parkinsonism [a brain disease], with any number of disabling conditions, it really is possible to have pleasure in life and to have a meaningful life if only one isn't depressed.[40]

Other experts, however, say that, although better hospice care and treatment for pain and depression would reduce the demand for assisted death, there will always be some patients whose suffering cannot be relieved. "Good comfort care and the availability of physician-assisted suicide are no more mutually exclusive than good cardiologic [heart] care and the availability of heart transplantation,"[41] Marcia Angell maintains.

A need for costly care

Better care is also needed for the much larger group of people who are incurably ill or disabled yet not dying. "We've made long-term care the step-child of medical care," says Joanne Lynn, a specialist in the care of the elderly and dying. "We've never properly funded [it]."[42] Lack of such care, forcing chronically ill people (those with long-lasting diseases) to lead miserable and lonely lives, has often proven to be the cause of their requests for assisted suicide or euthanasia. Opponents of assisted death believe that, if long-term care were improved,

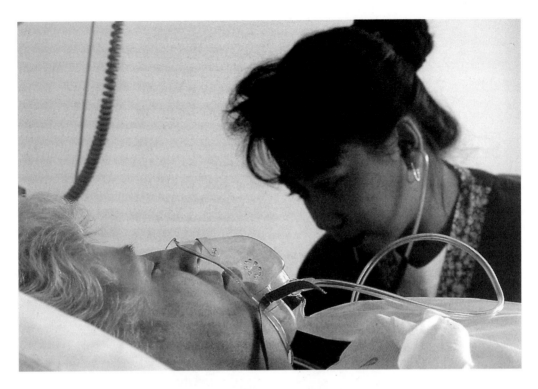

many of those who now ask for death would change their minds.

One of the chief problems that keeps many people from obtaining hospice care or, especially, chronic care—which may be needed for years or decades rather than hospice care's few months—is cost. Medicare, the insurance program funded by the federal government that pays part of medical costs for the nation's elderly, has covered hospice care since 1983. In 1998, however, Medicare officials were considering tightening the rules about paying for hospice and home care, claiming fraud and abuse in this rapidly growing part of the health care economy. In a time when insurance companies and health care institutions have become very concerned about costs, chronic care may be very hard to obtain. People who lack money or health insurance may find good care almost impossible to get, especially in the United States, which, unlike countries such as Canada, Britain, and the Netherlands, does not have a national system that provides health care to all of its citizens.

Many people believe patients need better care, not assisted suicide.

Teaching doctors about dying

Both supporters and opponents of letting doctors hasten death also agree that physicians and other health care professionals need better education about care for the dying. Until recently, many medical schools had no courses on palliative or end-of-life care, and schools that had such courses rarely required students to take them. As a result, even when effective treatments for pain or other problems exist,

Doctors are beginning to receive better education about care for the dying.

physicians may not know about them. They also may not know how to communicate with dying patients and discuss their wishes, including possible requests for assistance in dying. If doctors can find out why a patient has made such a request, they may be able to offer other ways of relieving suffering, such as helping the family obtain better home care. Medical schools and associations are now beginning to improve education in this area. In 1999, for instance, the American Medical Association began an extensive program to educate physicians in end-of-life care.

If physicians gain legal permission to assist patients' deaths under some circumstances, hospital ethics committees may help doctors make the difficult decision about whether to carry out such an action in particular cases. These groups, made up of physicians, clergy, ethicists, lawyers, social workers, and philosophers, have existed since the 1970s, and most hospitals now have them. At present, they review decisions about life-sustaining treatment, particularly when physicians and families disagree about whether treatment should be continued.

It is clear that people's thinking about what a physician should do for a dying patient is changing. Most people now agree that doctors should be allowed to let hopelessly ill patients die, but whether—and how—they should be permitted to help patients die is sure to be debated for a long time to come.

3

Euthanasia
and the Law

ALTHOUGH A FEW people like Jack Kevorkian may assist a terminally ill person's suicide or even commit euthanasia regardless of what the law says, most hesitate to perform actions that are illegal. A country's legislatures and courts therefore have a huge effect on what people do to control their own or others' deaths. Laws and court rulings made since the 1970s have played a major part in defining the "right" to die.

In the United States, courts so far have proved more willing to tackle this touchy subject than legislatures. In some two hundred rulings starting with the famous Karen Quinlan case in 1976, "the judiciary has transformed not only the practice of medicine and the rights of patients, but has also shaped societal values,"[43] Lawrence O. Gostin writes in the *Journal of the American Medical Association*.

The right to refuse treatment

Many court rulings have focused on the question of refusing medical treatment. From the beginning, judges have generally agreed that a competent adult has the right to refuse any treatment, even if doing so shortens or ends the person's life. This right is rooted in the basic right to control what happens to one's own body, which goes far back in American and British legal tradition. As the U.S. Supreme Court stated in 1891, "No right is held more sacred, or is more carefully guarded, by the common law, than the right of every individual to the possession and control of his own person [body]."[44]

The right to refuse treatment also arises from the definition of the crime called battery. Battery is any undesired touching not specifically permitted by law (such as being restrained by police during an arrest). Beginning in 1905, U.S. courts considered unwanted medical treatment to be a form of battery. A third part of the right to refuse treatment derives from the right to informed consent, which requires that a person be told about the risks and benefits of a medical procedure and about alternatives before deciding whether to accept the procedure.

A duty to preserve life

The law has been much less clear about how much right someone has to refuse life-sustaining care for someone else. Most of the important right-to-die court decisions in the 1970s and 1980s, including those in the cases of Karen Quinlan and Nancy Cruzan, dealt with this issue.

When people cannot make their own health care decisions, it seems reasonable to let family members or other appropriate surrogates make these decisions for them. On the other hand, judges have agreed that the government has a duty to preserve life and protect the helpless. When a surrogate's health care decision would end someone's life, therefore, the courts are likely to get involved. Judges try to ensure that such decisions are really in the patients' best interest.

The state's interest in protecting life won out over the surrogates' choice in the 1971 case of Delores Heston, a young woman who lost a great deal of blood in a car crash. Heston and her parents were Jehovah's Witnesses, a religious group that does not accept blood transfusions. Heston's parents, acting on her behalf because she was unconscious, denied Heston's hospital permission to give her a transfusion. The New Jersey Supreme Court, however, overruled them. The justices said that the government's interest outweighed the family's right to act on their religious views in this case because the transfusion would not only save Heston's life but would almost surely restore her to full health.

Five years later, the same court ruled the opposite way in the Karen Quinlan case. In this case, they said, the proposed treatment—the respirator—was expected to produce no change in Quinlan's permanent unconsciousness. "We think the state's interest [in preserving life] . . . weakens and the individual's right to privacy grows as the degree of bodily invasion increases and the prognosis [prediction of future health] dims,"[45] the justices wrote.

Determining wishes

In the Nancy Cruzan case in 1989–1990, both the Missouri and the U.S. Supreme Courts stressed the importance of trying to determine a formerly competent person's wishes before allowing a surrogate to act. Advance directives are an important way for people to express such wishes. In late 1990, five months after the Cruzan case was decided, Congress tried to encourage people to use ad-

vance directives and health care institutions to respect them by passing the Patient Self-Determination Act. This law requires all health care institutions that receive government funding (as most do) to inform new patients about their right to fill out advance directives and refuse medical treatments. The institutions must also tell the patients about the institutions' policies on these subjects.

The Patient Self-Determination Act has not proven to be enough, however. Several large studies have shown that even today, advance directives are often ignored. Several laws that would strengthen the Patient Self-Determination Act have been proposed, and some lawsuits against doctors and hospitals that insisted on treatment in spite of advance directives ordering its refusal have been successful. In the future, therefore, health care institutions may have to pay more attention to people's wishes, even when the people cannot speak for themselves.

Cases involving people who were never able to form ideas about health care have been hardest to decide. Some of the most wrenching ones involve children born with birth defects that severely limit their physical and mental development. Their doctors, parents, or both may believe that the best thing for them is to withhold all treatment, sometimes even including food and water, and let the babies die. Beginning in 1984, the federal government classified such nontreatment as child abuse. The only infants for whom treatment can be denied are those who are terminally ill, in irreversible comas, or suffering from conditions that make life support both futile and inhumane. Even in these cases, basic nutrition and liquids must be provided.

Defining a "right" to die

In the 1990s the focus of American courts shifted from people who wanted to refuse life-sustaining treatment to those who wanted to ask for a doctor's active help in dying. The question of whether terminally ill people have a constitutionally protected right to ask for such help was at the center of the decade's two most important right-to-die cases, which reached the Supreme Court together in 1997.

These cases began in 1994, when two groups, each made up of several physicians who treated the terminally ill and several anonymous terminally ill patients, filed suits claiming that state laws against assisted suicide violated the U.S. Constitution if they were applied to the terminally ill. One suit challenged a law in Washington State, the other in New York. Both were sponsored by Compassion in Dying, a Seattle-based organization that counsels terminally ill people and

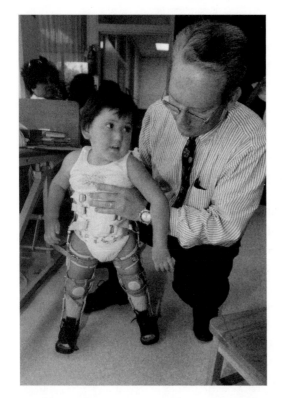

Though disabling for life, birth defects such as spina bifida cannot be grounds for withholding treatment.

their families. Compassion in Dying also joined directly in the Washington suit at first, although it withdrew later.

Almost every state in the United States, and most other Western countries as well, has a law like the ones these groups were trying to overthrow. Christianity and many other religions regard suicide as a sin, and for centuries both committing suicide and assisting another person to do so were against the law. Most states dropped the laws against committing suicide soon after the country's formation because people came to feel that these laws unfairly punished the families of those who committed suicide (the laws required that the dead person's property be forfeited to the government). Assisting a suicide, however, usually remained a crime, even if the person who died was incurably or terminally ill.

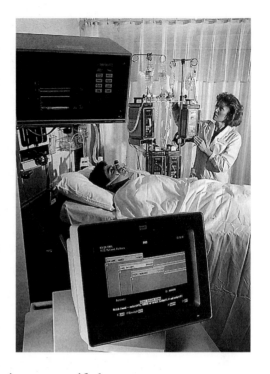

People in favor of assisted suicide claim that anti-euthanasia laws violate the Fourteenth Amendment.

In both of the 1994 lawsuits, the plaintiffs, or groups filing the suits, maintained that the state laws forbidding assistance in suicide violated two parts of the Fourteenth Amendment to the Constitution. One part, the due process clause, guarantees the right not to be deprived of life, liberty, or property without due process of law. Previous Supreme Court rulings had defined liberty as including the right to make certain private decisions, particularly ones related to bearing and raising children. The plaintiffs in the two suits claimed that decisions about the time and manner of a person's death were just as private and important as those about marriage and reproduction and thus were also protected under the due process clause.

In addition, the plaintiffs said that the laws against assisted suicide violated a second part of the Fourteenth Amendment, the equal protection clause. This clause guarantees equal protection of the law to everyone, meaning that laws must treat similar groups in the same way. A law cannot distinguish between men and women doing the same job, for instance. The plaintiffs maintained that terminally ill people whose lives were being sustained by medical devices were no different from terminally ill people who did not need such devices. By allowing the first group to hasten their deaths by refusing the devices but forbidding the second group to do so by obtaining a lethal prescription, they argued, the antisuicide laws treated these two similar groups differently and therefore violated the equal protection clause.

Attorneys for the states, in contrast, maintained that government interests outweighed any individual liberty interests protected by the due process clause. Besides the interest in preserving life, these state interests included preventing suicide, protecting the ethics of the medical profession by not allowing doctors to kill, and preventing abuse of vulnerable groups such as the elderly, the disabled, the poor, and minorities. The states' attorneys also claimed that actively ending life by a lethal prescription was significantly different from letting someone die by disconnecting a respirator or feeding tube. Therefore, terminally ill people demanding the first action were not similar to those demanding the second, so laws did not have to treat the two groups in the same way.

Controversial decisions

The Washington case, known first as *Compassion in Dying et al. v. State of Washington* and later as *Glucksberg v. Washington* (after Harold Glucksberg, a cancer specialist, who became the chief plaintiff after Compassion in Dying dropped out of the suit), was heard first in a federal district court in Seattle on May 3, 1994. Barbara Rothstein, the judge who heard the case, ruled that the Washington law violated both clauses of the Fourteenth Amendment.

The state appealed Rothstein's decision, and three judges from the federal Ninth Circuit Court of Appeals heard the case. Judge John T. Noonan Jr. delivered the court's majority ruling on March 9, 1995. Noonan reversed Rothstein's decision, saying that state interests outweighed any liberty interest that individuals might have in deciding to hasten their own deaths. Noonan and the other appeals court judge who sided with him were Catholics, however, so the right-to-die groups claimed that these judges might have been influenced by a religious bias against assisted suicide. The plaintiffs demanded a rehearing by the entire eleven-judge panel of the appeals court, and their request was granted on October 26, 1995.

On March 6, 1996, the Ninth Circuit Court of Appeals voted 8 to 3 to reverse Noonan's ruling. Judge Stephen Reinhardt, well known for his liberal opinions, delivered the court's majority opinion. Reinhardt agreed with Rothstein's conclusion that the Washington anti-assisted suicide law violated the due process clause of the Fourteenth Amendment. Reinhardt did not rule on whether the Washington law also violated the equal protection clause.

Like Rothstein, Reinhardt based his conclusion chiefly on a comparison with the right to make decisions about abortion. The Supreme Court had placed decisions about abortion among the private decisions protected by the due process clause in its famous 1973 ruling on the case of *Roe v. Wade* and reaffirmed that protection in a 1992 case, *Planned Parenthood of Southeastern Pennsylvania v. Casey*. In *Casey* the High Court justices wrote,

> These matters, involving the most intimate and personal choices a person may make in a lifetime, choices central to personal dignity and autonomy, are central to the liberty protected by the Fourteenth Amendment. At the heart of liberty is the right to define one's own concept of existence, of meaning, of the universe, and of the mystery of human life. Beliefs about these could not define the attributes of personhood were they formed under compulsion of the State.[46]

Rothstein and Reinhardt maintained that decisions about one's death were just as personal and important as decisions about bearing children and therefore should be similarly protected.

The New York suit followed a path similar to that of the Washington case. The leader in the physician-patient

Dr. Timothy Quill

group filing suit in New York was Timothy Quill, so the case was known as *Quill v. New York Attorney General,* or *Quill v. Vacco* (after Dennis C. Vacco, the New York attorney general at the time). Federal District Court judge Thomas Griesa ruled against the Quill group on December 15, 1994. In view of the long history of laws against assisting suicide in almost every state, he wrote, defining a right to assisted suicide as part of liberty interests protected by the Constitution did not make sense. He also maintained, as Noonan had, that there was an important "difference between allowing nature to take its course, even in the most severe situations, and intentionally using an artificial death-producing device."[47] Groups demanding these different treatments therefore were not similar enough to require equal legal treatment.

Quill's group appealed Griesa's decision, and three judges from the Second Circuit Court of Appeals reviewed the case. Judge Roger Miner delivered the appeals court's majority ruling on April 2, 1996. As Reinhardt had done in Washington less than a month earlier, Miner concluded that the state law against assisted suicide—at least as it applied to terminally ill people—violated the Fourteenth Amendment. Miner, however, focused on the equal protection clause rather than the due process clause. He upheld the claim of Quill and the others that terminally ill people who wanted to refuse life-sustaining treatment and those who wanted to ask for a physician's active help in dying were similar groups who were not treated similarly by the law. Letting someone die of hunger and thirst by removing a feeding tube, he maintained, was no more natural than giving a lethal prescription to a terminally ill person who asked for it.

The Supreme Court rules

Right-to-die supporters were delighted with Reinhardt's and Miner's rulings, but the states immediately appealed the decisions to the Supreme Court. The High Court heard the two cases, now known as *Washington State v. Glucksberg* and *New York State v. Quill*, on January 8, 1997. In addition to the arguments that lawyers for the opposing sides presented to the justices, sixty other individuals and groups submitted arguments for or against physician-assisted suicide in papers called *amicus curiae*, or friend of the court, briefs. Some of the groups, including the Hemlock Society and Not Dead Yet, a militant disabled-rights organization that strongly opposes legalization of physician-assisted suicide, also held demonstrations outside the courthouse.

On June 26, 1997, the Supreme Court justices agreed unanimously that the Washington and New York laws against assisting suicide were constitutional. Chief Justice

Members of Not Dead Yet protest against physician-assisted suicide.

William Rehnquist delivered the court's majority ruling. He saw no reason to reverse a type of law that was so widely accepted and had such a long tradition in the United States. Unlike Reinhardt, Rehnquist maintained that the government's interests in protecting life and preventing abuse of vulnerable people outweighed any possible individual "right" to die. He also held that, contrary to what Miner felt, people who wanted to refuse medical treatment and those who wanted assistance in suicide were not similar groups and thus were not entitled to similar treatment.

The Supreme Court decision was a major defeat for those who wanted to see physician-assisted suicide made legal, but it was not a complete one. The Court had suggested that state

Justice John Paul Stevens.

laws permitting assisted suicide were just as constitutional as those that denied it. Indeed, Rehnquist emphasized that the debate about assisted suicide was just beginning and that the states needed to experiment with different laws to discover which ones created the best balance between an individual's right to private decision making and the government's duty to protect its citizens.

Furthermore, several of the Supreme Court justices filed concurring opinions—opinions that agreed with the majority's main conclusion but did so for different reasons or offered different views of certain details. Some of these concurring opinions, especially the one by liberal justice John Paul Stevens, stated that, although the justices saw no overall constitutional right to die, they might uphold a right to assisted suicide in some particular situation presented in a future case.

Campaigns for new laws

While some right-to-die groups have fought in the courts to modify or remove existing laws against assisted suicide, others have tried to persuade legislators and voters to pass new laws that would permit physician-assisted suicide and euthanasia. The first attempt to legalize these acts was made in Ohio in 1906. The proposed bill would have allowed a physician to kill anyone who was incurably ill or injured and requested death in the presence of three witnesses. The bill failed to pass the legislative committee that reviewed it, however. The American Euthanasia Society, founded in 1938 to legalize assisted suicide and euthanasia, had no better luck. It tried several times to introduce its bill into the New York legislature but could never find a legislator willing to sponsor the controversial law.

Efforts to make assisted suicide, and, in some cases, euthanasia, legal for terminally ill people were revived in the 1990s. Derek Humphry's Hemlock Society led most of these campaigns, which all took place in western states and used the initiative process, in which a proposed law can be placed on the ballot for direct vote by the people.

The first of these modern attempts to legalize physician-assisted suicide and euthanasia took place in California in 1988, but the groups supporting the initiative could not gather enough signatures to qualify their measure for the ballot. Two other initiative measures, one in Washington State in 1991 and the other in California in 1992, did appear on voters' ballots, but they were ultimately just as unsuccessful.

Early polls suggested that a majority of voters favored the Washington and California measures, but groups who opposed the measures were powerful and well-funded. They included state medical associations as well as the Catholic Church and right-to-life groups, the latter two of which opposed assisted suicide and euthanasia for religious reasons. In both contests, opposition groups claimed that the measures did not include enough safeguards to prevent abuse. For example, they did not require a waiting period, which would give people who had requested suicide time to change their minds. They also included euthanasia, which could be done against someone's will. Both measures were defeated at the polls, with 46 percent of voters voting in favor of the measures and 54 percent against.

The Death with Dignity Act

A fourth attempt to legalize assisted death, made in Oregon in 1994, had better success. By then, groups favoring legalization had learned important lessons about what the American public would accept. Unlike the earlier measures, Oregon's Measure 16, the Death with Dignity Act, aimed to legalize only physician-assisted suicide, not euthanasia. It also permitted only prescriptions for lethal medication, not injections. This eliminated the mental image of a stealthy

Barbara Coombs Lee (second from right), supporter of Oregon's Death with Dignity Act, speaks to the media during the 1997 campaign to repeal the law.

doctor with a needle, which apparently had terrified many voters in the other states. The measure allowed only terminally ill, competent adults to request aid in dying. Finally, the Oregon measure included safeguards missing from the earlier ones, such as a waiting period, a requirement that two physicians verify the person's medical condition, and a requirement to have a psychiatrist examine the patient for depression if this mental illness were suspected.

On November 8, 1994, Oregon voters passed Measure 16 by a narrow margin, 52 percent in favor to 48 percent against. Just six hours before the Death with Dignity Act was scheduled to become law on December 5, however, its opponents persuaded Judge Michael Hogan to issue a temporary restraining order against it. Hogan made the restraining order permanent on August 4, 1995. He ruled that the law was unconstitutional because it denied the terminally ill the protection of existing laws against assisted suicide, thus violating the equal protection clause of the Fourteenth Amendment.

The Oregon law remained tied up in the courts until October 27, 1997, when the Ninth Circuit Court of Appeals reversed Hogan's ruling and allowed the Death with Dignity Act to go into effect. Oregon then became the first and, so far, only state in the United States to legalize physician-assisted suicide. By that time, however, the controversial law's opponents had placed a measure on the November ballot that, if passed, would have repealed the act. The repeal measure, Measure 51, failed by a much wider margin than that by which the original measure had passed, with 60 percent voting against it.

Congress steps in

Although they could not halt the Death with Dignity Act in Oregon, the law's foes drew a better response from some parts of the federal government. On November 5, the day after Measure 51's defeat, Thomas Constantine, head of the Drug Enforcement Administration, announced that any doctor prescribing controlled substances (which include narcotics and similar drugs) for suicide would violate the Controlled Substances Act. This statement in effect put the Oregon law on hold yet again until June 5, 1998, when U.S. Attorney General Janet Reno overruled Constantine.

U.S. Attorney General Janet Reno.

Opponents of assisted suicide felt that Reno had overstepped her authority. In response, Republican Senator Don Nickles of Oklahoma and Henry Hyde, a Republican representative from Illinois, introduced a bill called the Lethal Drug Abuse Prevention Act into the Senate and House of Representatives. If passed, the act would have made knowingly prescribing controlled substances for use in suicide a federal offense.

A number of medical and hospice associations objected to the proposed law. It would prevent doctors from using controlled substances to effectively treat severe pain, they complained, because the physicians would risk being sent to prison if their patients died. Because of this opposition, the act's sponsors withdrew and revised it. Their new version made a somewhat clearer distinction between the use of controlled substances for pain treatment—even in life-shortening doses—and for assisted suicide. It also added a $5-million appropriation for a program to improve pain management and palliative care.

Most of the medical groups said they were satisfied with these changes and removed their opposition to the bill. The revised act, now called the Pain Relief Promotion Act, was introduced into Congress in June 1999. The House of Representatives passed it on October 27.

Passage of the Pain Relief Promotion Act directly contradicted the Supreme Court's 1997 ruling, which returned the question of whether physician-assisted suicide and euthanasia should be made legal to the states. Chief Justice Rehnquist wrote in his majority opinion, "Throughout the Nation, Americans are engaged in an earnest and profound debate about the morality, legality and practicality of physician-assisted suicide. Our holding permits this debate to continue, as it should in a democratic society."[48] It remains to be seen whether Congress will also allow that debate or, instead, will take the decision out of state hands.

4

Experiments in Euthanasia

As PEOPLE TRY to guess what would happen if physician-assisted suicide and euthanasia were legalized, they look hard at the few places in the world where assisted suicide, euthanasia, or both are openly practiced. So far, there have been only three such places: Oregon, Australia's Northern Territory, and the Netherlands (Holland). All of these places have issued statistics about the physician-assisted deaths that have taken place in their regions. Interpreting this information, however, has proved to be anything but easy.

Oregon's first year

In February 1999 the Oregon Department of Health issued a report about the physician-assisted suicides that had taken place under the Death with Dignity Act during the law's first year of operation. Twenty-three terminally ill people received prescriptions for lethal drugs, the report stated—about a third of the number who requested such drugs. Fifteen of the twenty-three used the drugs to kill themselves. All of the suicides were successful, with most of the patients dying within an hour of taking the medication. Of the eight people who did not use their prescriptions, six died of their disease, and two were still alive as of January 1, 1999.

The average age of the patients was sixty-nine years. Eighteen of the twenty-three had cancer, an often painful

A cancer patient receives chemotherapy. The predicted rush to die among terminally ill patients did not occur in Oregon.

disease. Only one, however, gave uncontrollable pain as the chief reason for wanting to die. Most, instead, spoke of loss of dignity and independence. "Many physicians report that their patients had been decisive and independent throughout their lives or that the decision to request a lethal prescription was consistent with a long-standing belief about the importance of controlling the manner in which they died,"[49] the report stated. None of the patients mentioned concern about cost of care as a reason for seeking death.

Friends and foes of physician-assisted suicide interpreted this report in different ways. "It's what we expected—a year of impeccable [perfect] implementation,"[50] said Barbara Coombs Lee, coauthor and sponsor of the Oregon law. She and other supporters of the law noted that, contrary to the predictions of opposing groups, huge numbers of people had not rushed to die when assisted suicide became legal. The Oregon report also showed no sign of anyone having been coerced toward death and no failed suicide attempts, two other predictions that had been made during the repeal campaign.

Critics of assisted suicide, however, pointed out that all of the information in the report came from the physicians who wrote the lethal prescriptions. The patients' medical records were kept secret, so there was no way to check the truth of what the doctors said. There was also no way to find out whether other assisted suicides that did not follow the law's guidelines had taken place. End-of-life care expert Ezekiel J. Emanuel said the report suggested that

> either there is very little demand and hence little need for legalized physician-assisted suicide in the United States or there is a lot of euthanasia and physician-assisted suicide going on outside the law, undermining the notion that legalization is the only way to ensure regulation and enforcement of safeguards.[51]

Australia's experiment

A report from Australia's Northern Territory, which briefly experimented with legalizing physician-assisted suicide in 1996 and 1997, is equally hard to interpret. Australia consists of five states and three territories, of which the Northern Territory has the smallest population, about 180,000 people. In 1994 the territory's retiring minister, Marshall Perron, introduced a bill called the Rights of the Terminally Ill Act, which would permit physician-assisted suicide for terminally ill people who met certain requirements. As with the Oregon law, these included a waiting period and a requirement for the patient to be examined by two physicians. One physician had to be trained in treating depression. The patient had to be a competent, terminally ill adult who was experiencing "unacceptable" pain or suffering. Unlike the Oregon law, the Australian one required the physician assisting in suicide to be present at the time of death. Another difference was that the Australian law allowed lethal injections as well as prescriptions. Perron's bill passed the Northern Territory legislature by a one-vote margin in May 1995 and took effect on July 1, 1996.

The Rights of the Terminally Ill Act remained in effect for nine months. Many people opposed it, including advocates for the country's native people, the Aborigines, who made up about a third of the Northern Territory's population. Distrustful of a government that had often mistreated them, some Aborigines feared that the law would be used to kill them against their will if they entered a hospital. In September 1996 Kevin Andrews, a legislator from the state of Victoria, introduced the Euthanasia Laws Bill into the Australian Parliament (the equivalent of Congress in the United States). The bill was intended to repeal the Northern Territory law and forbade territories from passing such laws in the future. (Parliament has the right to strike down laws passed by territories, but it had never actually done so before.) Andrews's bill passed on March 24, 1997.

Although a poll taken in the Northern Territory soon after passage of the Rights of the Terminally Ill Act showed 46 percent of the Northern Territory's general population, 33 percent of nurses, and 14 percent of doctors in favor of it, only one physician actually offered to carry out assisted suicides under the law. He was Philip Nitschke, who has become known as Australia's equivalent of Jack Kevorkian. Nitschke said in early 1999 that he had helped sixty people die even after the Northern Territory law was repealed. He also planned to open a clinic in Melbourne to distribute information about euthanasia and assisted suicide.

While the Rights of the Terminally Ill Act was in effect, according to a report based on medical records and interviews with Nitschke, seven people asked to die under the law's provisions after it passed, and Nitschke helped four of them do so. (Two of the others died before the law went into effect, one by unassisted suicide and one of disease. The third died of terminal sedation after the law was repealed.) Nitschke used a drug-injecting

Dr. Philip Nitschke burns copies of an anti-euthanasia bill outside the Australian Federal Parliament in 1997.

machine somewhat similar to Kevorkian's Mercitron. The patient triggered it by clicking answers to questions on the screen of a laptop computer.

The first person to die under the Australian law—and thus the first person to commit legal physician-assisted suicide anywhere in the world—was sixty-six-year-old Bob Dent. Dent had cancer, as did the other six patients who requested death in the Northern Territory. (Doctors disagreed about whether some of the Australian patients were terminally ill, however.) The report on the Australian patients noted that three had few or no family members or friends to stand by them, and four showed some signs of depression. Thus, they may have had mental problems as well as physical ones.

Dr. Philip Nitschke became known as Australia's equivalent of Jack Kevorkian because of his willingness to help the terminally ill die.

The Netherlands: laboratory of euthanasia

It is hard to draw conclusions from the reports from Oregon and Australia because they involve such small numbers of people. So to really understand what happens when physician-assisted suicide and euthanasia become widespread, observers turn to the one country where these actions take place openly and fairly commonly: the Netherlands. That country, says medical ethicist Edmund Pellegrino, is "a living laboratory of what happens when a society accepts the legitimacy of [physician-assisted suicide and euthanasia]. You've got direct . . . evidence."[52]

Physician-assisted suicide and euthanasia are not actually legal in the Netherlands. Doctors are seldom prosecuted for carrying them out, however, and are almost never punished. The argument for allowing physicians to commit technically illegal actions without penalty is that the doctors perform these deeds under "necessity or duress"[53] arising from their duty to prevent suffering.

This strange situation began in 1973 when Geertruida Postma, a Dutch physician, was charged with murder after giving her elderly mother a fatal injection. The mother was terminally ill and had requested the injection, Postma said during her highly publicized trial. Postma was found guilty but given only a brief suspended sentence and a year's probation. In 1984, following a Dutch Supreme Court decision, government attorneys agreed not to prosecute doctors who assisted in suicide or committed euthanasia if they followed guidelines drawn up by the Royal Dutch Medical Association. The Ministry of Justice made the agreement official in 1990.

The Dutch medical guidelines are generally similar to those in Oregon and Australia, but with some important differences. They require that a patient make clear, repeated requests for assisted suicide or euthanasia (although the guidelines were revised in 1994 to allow involuntary euthanasia under some circumstances) and be experiencing unbearable, unrelievable suffering. Two doctors must examine the patient, and the physician committing the act must report it to legal authorities. Unlike the cases in Oregon and Australia, however, a Dutch patient asking for help in dying does not have to be terminally or even physically ill. The Dutch guidelines permit both assisted suicide and euthanasia, but the Dutch apparently prefer euthanasia because it produces a quicker and surer death.

The Remmelink reports

Because of great interest in the Dutch experience with assisted death, the government of the Netherlands has issued two reports on physician-assisted suicide and euthanasia in that country. The first, called the Remmelink Report, was issued in 1991 and provided statistics for 1990. Information for the report was gathered both from coroners' files and from questionnaires that physicians filled out anonymously. The questionnaires were needed because investigators found that a high percentage of doctor-caused deaths were not reported to authorities, even though the guidelines required this.

The Remmelink Report stated that of about 130,000 total deaths in the Netherlands in 1990, 2,300 (1.8 percent) were caused by voluntary euthanasia and 400 (0.3 percent) by physician-assisted suicide. More than 99 percent of the patients dying this way were said to be terminally ill. Only about a third of the people who requested aid in dying were granted it, the report said. Terminal sedation caused or contributed to an additional 1,350 deaths (1 percent).

The most disturbing category to many observers was one defined as "euthanasia without request by the patient." Some 1,000 deaths (0.8 percent of the total) fell into this group.

According to the doctors who caused these deaths, 79 percent of the patients were incompetent to request or consent at the time the decision for euthanasia was made. The doctors claimed that more than half of these patients had requested death at an earlier time. The doctors said they had talked to family members or other physicians about their decisions when incompetent patients had left no clear wishes. The report did not explain why the physicians had not discussed euthanasia with the patients before carrying it out in the 21 percent of cases in which the patients were competent to make health care decisions.

To answer questions raised by the original report and to find out whether the practice of physician-assisted suicide and euthanasia had been changing, the Dutch government issued a second report in 1995. This account found that, although the percentage of reported deaths from physician-assisted suicide and euthanasia had gone up, the total number of estimated deaths had not changed by much. The report also stated that 3,200 to 3,600 people had died from voluntary euthanasia and that the number of involuntary euthanasia cases had dropped from 1,000 to 900.

Sliding down a slippery slope?

To an even greater extent than with the Oregon and Australia reports, different observers drew widely contrasting conclusions from the Remmelink reports' figures. Pointing to small changes in the numbers of deaths in each category of assisted dying, the authors of the second report concluded that there were "no signs of an unacceptable increase in the number of decisions [to commit euthanasia] or of less careful decision making"[54] by Dutch doctors between 1990 and 1995. Replying to critics who had claimed that the Netherlands was sliding down a "slippery slope" from voluntary to involuntary euthanasia, the authors claimed that the statistics "do not support the idea that physicians in the Netherlands are moving down a slippery slope."[55]

Critics of euthanasia such as Herbert Hendin, director of the American Foundation for Suicide Prevention, came to exactly the opposite conclusion. Hendin compared the two

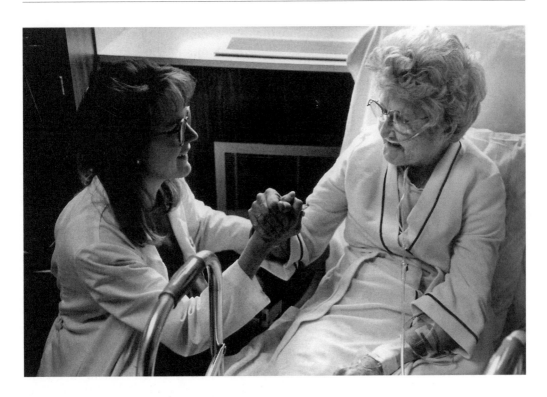

reports' statistics by looking at the amount of change as a percentage of the lower figure. He pointed out that voluntary euthanasia deaths increased by 40% over a five year period—from 2,300 in 1990 to 3,200 in 1995. Looked at in this way, the changes seemed much larger. "The reports . . . provide ample evidence that the slippery slope is no myth but a reality,"[56] concluded fellow critic Edmund Pellegrino.

A doctor comforts an elderly patient. Although euthanasia is illegal in the Netherlands, Dutch doctors are rarely prosecuted for helping their patients die.

The increase in the number of doctor-assisted deaths was not the only problem that Hendin and others found in the Dutch reports. "Virtually every guideline established by the Dutch to regulate euthanasia has been modified or violated with impunity [no punishment],"[57] Hendin says. The reporting requirement was ignored most often. Many doctors also did not ask other physicians to examine their patients, perhaps because the murky legal status of assisted suicide and euthanasia made them unsure how open they could be about these actions. Critics of physician-assisted suicide believe that guidelines included in laws like Oregon's are likely to be similarly ignored.

Hendin and even some Dutch doctors worry about the tremendous power—literally the power of life and death—that the Netherlands' system gives physicians. "Doctors determine how euthanasia is practiced, they establish the diagnosis [decide what illness the person has], they inform the patient if they want, they decide whether to report [the death] to the authorities—and most cases are not reported,"[58] says Richard Fenigsen, a retired Dutch physician who has become an opponent of euthanasia. Hendin offers some disturbing examples in which physicians seem to have abused their power. One doctor, for instance, euthanized a woman with advanced cancer against her will because "it could have taken another week before she died. I . . . needed this [hospital] bed."[59]

Euthanasia for mental distress

Another part of the Dutch practice that distresses critics like Hendin is the broadening categories of people considered eligible for physician-assisted suicide and euthanasia. As Hendin wrote in 1997,

> The Netherlands has moved from . . . euthanasia for terminally ill patients to euthanasia for those who are chronically ill, from euthanasia for physical illness to euthanasia for psychological distress, and from voluntary euthanasia to nonvoluntary and involuntary euthanasia.[60]

One of the most disturbing examples came to light in 1994, when Dutch psychiatrist Boudewijn Chabot went on trial for giving a prescription for lethal drugs to a fifty-year-old woman named Hilly Bosscher. Bosscher never claimed that she suffered from any physical illness; rather, she was severely depressed because of the deaths of her two sons and years of abuse from her alcoholic husband.

Chabot tried to treat Bosscher's depression when she first came to him and asked for help in dying. After several months, however, she said that the treatment was not helping her and repeated her earlier request. Chabot described Bosscher's case to seven other doctors and asked their opinions, but none of them actually examined Bosscher. The Dutch Supreme Court convicted Chabot of violating the medical guidelines because of this lack of examination, but he was not punished.

The Dutch guidelines had never required that a patient have a physical illness, but Bosscher's case was the first widely publicized one in which a lethal prescription had been given to someone whose only problem was psychological. "The [court] ruling recognizes the right of patients experiencing severe psychic pain to choose to die with dignity,"[61] Chabot's attorney maintained. Most people in the United States who heard of the case were shocked by it, however, just as many had been shocked to learn that some people whom Jack Kevorkian had helped to die apparently had not been physically ill either. (Unlike Chabot and Bosscher, however, Kevorkian and his patients were not aware of this.)

Although Kevorkian did not realize it, some of his patients were not physically ill at the time of their deaths.

Famed American ethicist Arthur Caplan said that allowing assisted suicide for mental suffering alone "is a morally frightening place for the public policy of any nation to be."[62]

The Dutch themselves have mixed feelings about their system. Polls show that most citizens—about 80 percent by 1996—approve of letting physicians provide euthanasia to terminally ill people at the patients' request. Nonetheless, some elderly and disabled people worry that they may be killed without their consent or that of their families. A group of severely disabled people expressed this fear in a letter to the Dutch government in the early 1990s: "We feel our lives threatened. . . . We realize that we cost the community a lot. . . . Many people think we are useless. . . . Often we notice that we are being talked into desiring death."[63] Some Dutch citizens carry "life passports" stating that they do not want euthanasia if they are admitted to a hospital while incompetent.

The Netherlands and the United States

Even if the Dutch system worked perfectly in its homeland, many observers doubt that it would function as well in the United States because of major differences between the two countries. "For goodness sakes, don't [try to imitate the Netherlands' system]," Dutch physician Herbert Cohen warns American policymakers. "You'll be in trouble."[64] Perhaps the most important difference is the fact that the Netherlands has a national health system that guarantees care to all citizens, whereas the United States does not. People in the Netherlands, therefore, are unlikely to want to kill themselves because they cannot receive the health care they need. This may not be so in the United States. Physicians in the Netherlands are also much more likely to have close, long-term relationships with their patients than American doctors are. Therefore, they have a better chance of understanding their patients' needs and states of mind.

People in the Netherlands, furthermore, are much more similar to each other in race, class, income, and culture than are the diverse citizens of the United States. They are thus more likely to have similar opinions on subjects such as euthanasia. When their opinions do differ, they pride themselves on having open, calm discussions rather than the protests and name calling that sometimes mark clashes between different groups in America. For all of these reasons, critics believe that abuse of physician-assisted suicide and euthanasia is more likely in the United States than it is in the Netherlands—which critics claim already has enough abuse of its own.

Evidence from the few experiments in euthanasia that have taken place is anything but clear-cut. The many different interpretations of the data from Oregon, Australia, and the Netherlands show that people see what they want or expect to see when they look at these figures. Nonetheless, reports from these places are probably the best guides available for predicting what might happen if physician-assisted suicide and euthanasia ever become common in the United States.

5

A Duty to Die?

Some experts believe that the euthanasia debate is over; others contend that an aging population only makes the argument more intense.

WHAT WILL HAPPEN to the debate about physician-assisted suicide and euthanasia in the twenty-first century? Will interest in this issue die down or grow? How will changes in medicine and society change people's feelings about it?

Some experts think the debate has served its purpose and therefore will become less important in the future. "The clamor for euthanasia and physician-assisted suicide pushed

medical professionals to improve end-of-life care," says Ezekiel J. Emanuel. "With those changes established, the assisted-suicide movement itself may be in terminal condition."[65] Others, however, think that as the world's population continues to grow and an ever-increasing number of people live into old age, arguments about the right to die will become more intense. Burke Baulche, director of the department of medical ethics at the National Right to Life Committee, says, "There is no question that the struggle over euthanasia will be one of the most dominant issues into the [twenty-first] century."[66]

Surveys in the late 1990s suggested that two-thirds to three-fourths of the public in the United States, Canada, Britain, and similar countries favored some form of assisted death, under some circumstances. About half of the countries' doctors felt the same. It therefore seems fairly possible that assisted dying will eventually be legalized to some degree. Even if it is not, some patients will no doubt continue to ask for it, and some doctors will still carry it out in secret. Figures from 1995 indicated that doctors in Washington State, where assisted suicide and euthanasia were illegal, and in the Netherlands, where they were legal in all but name, received requests for aid in dying about equally often. Doctors in both places granted about an equal percentage of these requests. These facts suggest that the legal status of assisted dying may not really matter.

A tradition of independence

What might America's future be if physician-assisted suicide and euthanasia were to become legal or, at least, were practiced as widely as they are in the Netherlands? In trying to guess the answer to this question, commentators look at the attitudes and values of today's society. They also consider ways in which society seems likely to change in the near future.

The United States was founded on a tradition of liberty, a belief that people should be able to do what they wish as long as they do not hurt others. Americans pride themselves on their independence and ability to take care of themselves. They value their right to make decisions about their own lives, including health care decisions, sometimes more highly than anything else. Most other Western democracies have similar values. "One of the most important ethical principles in medicine is respect for each patient's autonomy [self-determination]," writes *New England Journal of Medicine* editor Marcia Angell. "When this principle conflicts with others, it should almost always take precedence [come first]."[67]

Over and over, both right-to-die supporters and patients who ask for assisted death have stressed how important self-reliance is to them. Many feel that the dependency and weakness created by serious or terminal illnesses are truly worse than death. Although right-to-die groups have usually described uncontrollable pain as the chief reason a

Twentieth-century American feminist and author Charlotte Perkins Gilman (center) killed herself to avoid a painful death from cancer.

sick person might want to die, study after study has shown that the most common actual reasons are fear of loss of dignity and of being a burden to their families.

Many Washington State physicians surveyed in 1995, for example, said that the most frequent concerns expressed by patients asking for help in dying were losing control, being a burden, being dependent, and losing dignity. Only about half of the patients said they were worried about pain or other major physical discomfort. "Their concerns underscore the importance of autonomy and self-determination for patients who want death to be hastened,"[68] the study's authors wrote. As Charlotte Perkins Gilman, an early twentieth-century American feminist, wrote shortly before she killed herself to avoid a slow death from cancer in 1935, "The record of a previously noble life is precisely what makes it sheer insult to allow death in pitiful degradation. We may not wish to 'die with our boots on,' but we may well prefer to 'die with our brains on.'"[69]

A "culture of death"?

Many observers feel that if the terminally ill were allowed to receive help in dying, society's stress on autonomy and self-reliance would almost guarantee that that "right" would in time be extended to the incurably ill or disabled, the elderly, and, indeed, almost anyone who wanted it, just as has happened in the Netherlands. After all, why should only the terminally ill be allowed to make decisions about the quality of their lives? Some right-to-die groups in fact have already extended their concerns beyond the terminally ill. On October 19, 1998, for example, the World Federation of Right-to-Die Societies issued a declaration stating that people "suffering severe and enduring distress [should be able] to receive medical help to die,"[70] whether or not they are terminally ill.

If this happens, critics of the right-to-die movement say, these same people—the incurably sick, the disabled, and the elderly—could be in danger from the healthy members of society because they are in the devalued condition of being dependent. Leo Alexander, an investigator for the Nazi war

Some critics believe that legalizing any euthanasia programs could lead to atrocities like the Holocaust.

crimes trials in Nuremberg, wrote in 1949 that all of the Nazi atrocities, including the Holocaust,

> started with [German physicians'] acceptance of the attitude, basic in the euthanasia movement, that there is such a thing as life not worthy to be lived. This attitude in its early stages concerned itself merely with the severely and chronically sick. Gradually the sphere of those to be included in this category was enlarged to encompass the socially unproductive, the ideologically unwanted, the racially unwanted and finally all non-Germans. But it is important to realize that the infinitely small wedged-in lever from which this entire trend of mind received its impetus [start] was the attitude toward the nonrehabilitable sick.[71]

Pope John Paul II sees a similar attitude creating what he calls a "culture of death" today. He said in 1995,

> This culture is actively fostered by powerful cultural, economic and political currents which encourage an idea of society excessively concerned with efficiency. . . . A person who, because of illness, handicap or, more simply, just by existing, compromises the well-being or lifestyle of those who are more favored tends to be looked upon as an enemy to be resisted or eliminated.[72]

Threats to the disabled

Some disabled people and their advocates have also said that they are afraid of what might happen if physician-assisted suicide and euthanasia were to become available to people who are not terminally ill. Bob Joondeph, a spokesman for the Oregon Advocacy Center for the disabled, told the Oregon legislature when it was considering bills to repeal the Death with Dignity Act in 1997, "People with disabilities have a well-founded fear of euthanasia. Historically, people with disabilities have been the first to be sacrificed to social imperatives of purity or utility."[73] Disabled people in the Netherlands have expressed similar fears. Other undervalued groups would soon join the disabled in death, predicts Rabbi A. James Rudin: "In the real medical world, the first people who will be assisted in ending their lives will be the poor, those without family or friends, the elderly, the disabled and uninsured patients who cannot pay for their medical treatments."[74]

Valuing independence above all other personal qualities can also affect a disabled person's view of his or her own life. "What makes life with a major physical disability ignominious [dishonorable], embarrassing, humiliating, and dehumanizing," disability advocate Paul Longmore wrote in 1987, "is not the need for extensive physical assistance, but the dehumanizing social contempt toward those who require such aid."[75] Acceptance of this low value can make some disabled people consider suicide. Many of the people who asked Jack Kevorkian for help in dying were disabled or incurably, but not terminally, ill. Similarly, several severely disabled people in the 1980s made highly publicized attempts to have the courts force hospitals to help them kill themselves. More might make such requests if physician-assisted suicide and euthanasia are legalized and the right to request them is extended beyond the terminally ill.

Members of Not Dead Yet demonstrate outside the Supreme Court in 1987.

The way to avoid this threat, disability advocates and disabled people themselves say, is to improve services for the disabled and, above all, change society's attitude toward disability. Advocates point out that although the courts in the 1980s ultimately granted the disabled people their wish to die, they never used the permission they had fought so hard to gain. Publicity surrounding their court appearances put them in touch with others who improved their lives enough to make them give up their plans for suicide. Many of the disabled people who are currently considering assisted suicide or euthanasia might similarly change their minds if given more respect and better services. "We don't want to die," says Diane Coleman, a leader of the disabled rights group Not Dead Yet. "We want health care and community-based services so we can live."[76]

Dying to save money

The risk that disabled and elderly people will be pressured to choose assisted death is increased by the problem of rising health care costs. This problem, which is already severe, will likely worsen in the future as the elderly populations in industrialized countries continue to grow. One out of eight Americans is over sixty-five years old today, and that proportion is expected to rise to one out of every four or five—close to 70 million people—by the year 2030. The elderly usually need more medical services than the young, so the demand for health care is likely to grow as the population ages.

Attempts to control costs have already reorganized health care in ways that limit care for some people, especially those who cannot afford private health insurance. Some critics worry about how this stress on saving money could affect the way physician-assisted suicide and euthanasia might be used if they were legalized. "We're talking about cutting Medicare and our social obligation to take care of the disabled, and at the same time we're also talking about physician-assisted suicide, and no one's noticing that they might come together in a very difficult way,"[77] says Joanne Lynn, a specialist in care of the elderly and chronically ill.

Some people worry that elderly patients may be pressured to choose assisted death as a result of rising health costs.

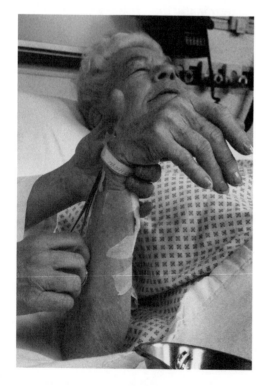

Health care organizations might promote assisted suicide and euthanasia as a way to cut costs, predicts New York attorney general Dennis Vacco. A lethal prescription or injection, after all, is far less expensive than several months of hospice care, let alone years or decades of care for the chronically ill or incurably disabled. In 1997 the respected New York Task Force on Life and the Law concluded that

> the chief problem with assisted suicide may not be moral and legal so much as financial: it is just too cheap relative to the available medical alternatives. And, in a world of market medicine and tightening government budgets, cheap is all too likely to mean attractive.[78]

A right could become a duty

In short, some advocates for the elderly and disabled fear that, if what is now called a "right" to die is legally recognized, it may become a "duty" to die as pressure on the health care system increases. Attorneys Robert P. George and William C. Porth Jr. wrote in 1995,

> As our population ages, government will face increased burdens in caring for the elderly. It is not unrealistic to fear that government may assume what began as a private prerogative [right], and move from making life-and-death decisions for the comatose, to making them for the insane, for the retarded, for those of less-than-average intelligence, and finally for those who are entirely rational and intelligent, but whose desire to cling to life brands them as obstinate, uncooperative, and just plain unreasonable.[79]

Instead of having to plead with authorities for permission to end their lives, critics of assisted suicide say, the elderly, sick, and disabled might someday have to plead for permission to continue their lives.

People protest an assisted-suicide bill in Sacramento, California.

Support for these fears comes from the fact that some right-to-die advocates, such as Derek Humphry, have recently stated that severely sick people, especially if they are also elderly, may indeed sometimes have a duty to end their lives in order to conserve health care resources for society as a whole. Humphry and Mary Clement wrote in 1998,

> The undeniable truth is that the elderly are putting a strain on the health care system that will only increase and cannot be sustained. . . . This disproportionate spending is leading some to consider right-to-die possibilities for relief. . . . A new study of seriously ill people in hospitals found that 30 percent of those surveyed said they would rather *die* than live permanently in a nursing home. This information begs the question: Why do we, as a nation, not allow these people to die . . . ? Their lives would conclude with dignity and self-respect, and one measure of cost containment would be in place.[80]

Will safeguards like those written into the Oregon assisted-suicide law be enough to prevent most of this abuse? Right-to-die supporters say yes. They point out that people today could be pressured into discontinuing medical treatment, yet there is little evidence that this occurs frequently. "The way to deal with these risks is not to prohibit this practice but to regulate it,"[81] says Alan Meisel, director of the University of Pittsburgh's Center for Medical Ethics.

The euthanasia debate has raised interest in conditions and care for the elderly and terminally ill.

Critics, however, say that these safeguards would be hard to enforce. They believe that allowing even those who are terminally ill and suffering terribly to demand an end to their lives will make society begin sliding down a "slippery slope," with Nazi-style forced euthanasia waiting at the bottom. "Once the turn has been made down the road to euthanasia, [it] could soon turn into a convenient and commodious [spacious] expressway,"[82] respected ethicist Daniel Callahan, founder of the Hastings Center, has warned. *New England Journal of Medicine* editor Marcia Angell replies, "It is impossible to avoid slippery slopes in medicine (or in any aspect of life). . . . The question is not whether a perfect system can be devised, but whether abuses are likely to be sufficiently rare to be offset by the benefits."[83]

A need for debate

No matter what is eventually decided about physician-assisted suicide and euthanasia—and there will most likely be many decisions in different times and places—people have a hard debate ahead of them. Thoughtful debate, controlled by reason rather than emotion, is just what the issue needs, says Thomas A. Shannon of the Worcester Polytechnic Institute in Massachusetts:

> The prolonged public debate served to clarify the issues and helped establish a national consensus which supported the removal of therapies [medical treatments] that prolonged life but provided few other benefits. While the process was long and extremely painful for the patients' families, the nation benefited because there was no fast resolution. . . . Only a genuine national, popular debate can benefit the resolution of this issue [assisted suicide and euthanasia].[84]

The debate over physician-assisted suicide and euthanasia has already produced positive results. It has brought people's attention to problems that limit care of the dying and treatment of the sick, the elderly, and the disabled. It has helped to start health care providers and governments on the road to solving those problems. With luck, however this debate is resolved, it will help an ever-growing number of people achieve both a "good death" and a good life.

Notes

Introduction

1. Quoted in Derek Humphry and Ann Wickett, *The Right to Die: An Historical and Legal Perspective of Euthanasia.* Eugene, OR: Hemlock Society, 1990, p. 8.

2. David Heim, "Being Creatures," *Christian Century*, July 17–24, 1996, p. 707.

3. Quoted in Maureen Harrison and Steve Gilbert, eds., *Life, Death, and the Law*. San Diego: Excellent Books, 1997, p. 73.

Chapter 1: Changing Attitudes

4. Quoted in Steve Hallock, "Physician-Assisted Suicide: 'Slippery Slope' or Civil Right?" *Humanist*, July-August 1996, p. 8.

5. Quoted in Derek Humphry and Mary Clement, *Freedom to Die: People, Politics, and the Right-to-Die Movement.* New York: St. Martin's, 1998, p. 19.

6. Quoted in Peter G. Filene, *In the Arms of Others: A Cultural History of the Right-to-Die in America.* Chicago: Ivan R. Dee, 1998, p. 65.

7. Quoted in Humphry and Wickett, *The Right to Die*, p. 91.

8. Quoted in Filene, *In the Arms of Others*, p. 127.

9. Quoted in Humphry and Clement, *Freedom to Die*, p. 88.

10. Quoted in Filene, *In the Arms of Others*, p. 104.

11. Quoted in Filene, *In the Arms of Others*, p. 162.

12. Quoted in Harrison and Gilbert, *Life, Death, and the Law*, p. 20.

13. Quoted in Harrison and Gilbert, *Life, Death, and the Law*, p. 26.

14. Quoted in Harrison and Gilbert, *Life, Death, and the Law*, p. 28.

15. Quoted in Humphry and Wickett, *The Right to Die*, p. 116.

16. Quoted in Humphry and Wickett, *The Right to Die*, p. 117.

17. Gary L. Thomas, "Deadly Compassion," *Christianity Today*, June 16, 1997, p. 14ff.

18. John M. Benson, "The Polls–Trends on End-of-Life Issues," *Public Opinion Quarterly*, Summer 1999, p. 263ff.

Chapter 2: Doctors and Death

19. Quoted in Gregory E. Pence, *Classic Cases in Medical Ethics*. New York: McGraw-Hill, 1995, p. 63.

20. Quoted in Pence, *Classic Cases in Medical Ethics*, p. 63.

21. Quoted in Filene, *In the Arms of Others*, p. 189.

22. Quoted in Sue Woodman, *Last Rights: The Struggle over the Right to Die*. New York: Plenum, 1998, p. 96.

23. Quoted in Pence, *Classic Cases in Medical Ethics*, p. 85.

24. Woodman, *Last Rights*, p. 91.

25. Quoted in Pence, *Classic Cases in Medical Ethics*, p. 71.

26. Quoted in Humphry and Clement, *Freedom to Die*, p. 126.

27. Quoted in Filene, *In the Arms of Others*, pp. 190–191.

28. Quoted in Jessica Cooper, "Consider Yourself Stopped," *National Right to Life News*, May 11, 1999, p. 12.

29. Quoted in Woodman, *Last Rights*, p. 180.

30. Quoted in Humphry and Clement, *Freedom to Die*, p. 276.

31. Humphry and Clement, *Freedom to Die*, p. 142.

32. Quoted in Woodman, *Last Rights*, p. 174.

33. Quoted in Jerry Filteau, "Suicide Ruling Spurs Wide Opposition," *National Catholic Reporter*, March 22, 1996, p. 4.

34. Quoted in Ezekiel Emanuel, "Whose Right to Die?" *Atlantic Monthly*, March 1997, p. 78.

35. Quoted in Harrison and Gilbert, *Life, Death, and the Law*, p. 175.

36. Marcia Angell, "The Supreme Court and Physician-Assisted Suicide—the Ultimate Right," *New England Journal of Medicine*, January 2, 1997, p. 51.

37. Angell, "The Supreme Court and Physician-Assisted Suicide," p. 52.

38. Quoted in Paul Cotton, "Medicine's Position Is Both Pivotal and Precarious in Assisted-Suicide Debate," *Journal of the American Medical Association*, February 1, 1995, p. 362.

39. Quoted in Humphry and Clement, *Freedom to Die*, p. 50.

40. Quoted in Sara Rimer, "Focus on Seniors' Depression," *New York Times*, reprinted in *San Francisco Examiner*, September 5, 1999.

41. Angell, "The Supreme Court and Physician-Assisted Suicide," p. 51.

42. Quoted in Thomas, "Deadly Compassion," p. 18.

Chapter 3: Euthanasia and the Law

43. Lawrence O. Gostin, "Deciding Life and Death in the Courtroom," *Journal of the American Medical Association*, November 12, 1997, p. 1523.

44. Quoted in Gostin, "Deciding Life and Death in the Courtroom," p. 1523.

45. Quoted in Albert R. Jonsen, Robert M. Veatch, and LeRoy Walters, eds., *Source Book in Bioethics: A Documentary History*. Washington, D.C.: Georgetown University Press, 1998, p. 146.

46. Quoted in Harrison and Gilbert, *Life, Death, and the Law*, p. 46.

47. Quoted in Harrison and Gilbert, *Life, Death, and the Law*, p. 153.

48. Quoted in Harrison and Gilbert, *Life, Death, and the Law*, p. 199.

Chapter 4: Experiments in Euthanasia

49. Quoted in Associated Press, "Fifteen Assisted Suicides Under New Oregon Law," *San Francisco Chronicle*, February 18, 1999, p. A3.

50. Quoted in Associated Press, "Fifteen Assisted Suicides Under New Oregon Law," p. A3.

51. Ezekiel J. Emanuel, "The End of Euthanasia? Death's Door," *New Republic*, May 17, 1999, p. 16.

52. Quoted in Thomas, "Deadly Compassion," pp. 14ff.

53. Quoted in Humphry and Clement, *Freedom to Die*, p. 143.

54. Paul J. van der Maas et al., "Euthanasia, Physician-Assisted Suicide, and Other Medical Practice Involving the End of Life in the Netherlands, 1990–1995," *New England Journal of Medicine*, November 28, 1996, p. 1699.

55. Van der Maas, "Euthanasia, Physician-Assisted Suicide, and Other Medical Practice Involving the End of Life in the Netherlands, 1990–1995," p. 1705.

56. Quoted in Thomas, "Deadly Compassion," pp. 14ff.

57. Quoted in Paul Wilkes, "The Next Pro-Lifers," *New York Times Magazine*, July 21, 1996, p. 26.

58. Joseph P. Shapiro with David Bowermaster, "Death on Trial," *U.S. News & World Report*, April 25, 1994, p. 36.

59. Quoted in Herbert Hendin, Chris Rutenfrans, and Zbigniew Zylicz, "Physician-Assisted Suicide and Euthanasia in the Netherlands: Lessons from the Dutch," *Journal of the American Medical Association*, June 4, 1997, pp. 1720ff.

60. Hendin, Rutenfrans, and Zylicz, "Physician-Assisted Suicide and Euthanasia in the Netherlands," pp. 1720ff.

61. Quoted in Randall E. Otto, "Bottom of the Slope," *Commonweal*, May 19, 1995, pp. 5–6.

62. Quoted in Humphry and Clement, *Freedom to Die*, p. 150.

63. Quoted in Michael Fumento, "Euthanasia in Netherlands Is Cautionary Tale for U.S.," *Insight on the News*, April 17, 1995, pp. 34–35.

64. Quoted in Joseph P. Shapiro, "Euthanasia's Home: What the Dutch Experience Can Teach Americans About Assisted Suicide," *U.S. News & World Report*, January 13, 1997, p. 24.

Chapter 5: A Duty to Die?

65. Emanuel, "The End of Euthanasia?" p. 16.

66. Quoted in Woodman, *Last Rights*, p. 214.

67. Angell, "The Supreme Court and Physician-Assisted Suicide," p. 50.

68. Anthony L. Back et al., "Physician-Assisted Suicide and Euthanasia in Washington State," *Journal of the American Medical Association*, March 27, 1996, p. 924.

69. Quoted in Pence, *Classic Cases in Medical Ethics*, p. 41.

70. Quoted in Wesley J. Smith, "Assisted Suicide Isn't 'Death with Dignity,'" *San Francisco Chronicle*, November 12, 1998.

71. Quoted in Humphry and Wickett, *The Right to Die*, p. 27.

72. Pope John Paul II, "Excerpts from *Evangelium Vitae*," *National Catholic Reporter*, April 7, 1995, p. 4.

73. Quoted in Humphry and Clement, *Freedom to Die*, p. 238.

74. Quoted in *Christian Century*, "Foes of Assisted Suicide Marshal Arguments," March 19, 1997, p. 288.

75. Quoted in Pence, *Classic Cases in Medical Ethics*, p. 57.

76. Quoted in Kathi Wolfe, "Disabled Activists Fight Assisted Suicide," *Progressive*, September 1996, p. 16.

77. Quoted in Thomas, "Deadly Compassion," p. 14ff.

78. Quoted in Michael Walzer, "Feed the Face," *New Republic*, June 9, 1997, p. 29.

79. Robert P. George and William C. Porth Jr., "Death, Be Not Proud," *National Review*, June 26, 1995, p. 52.

80. Humphry and Clement, *Freedom to Die*, pp. 316, 319.

81. Quoted in Hallock, "Physician-Assisted Suicide," p. 11.

82. Quoted in Filene, *In the Arms of Others*, p. 192.

83. Angell, "The Supreme Court and Physician-Assisted Suicide," pp. 51–52.

84. Thomas A. Shannon, "Physician-Assisted Suicide: Ten Questions," *Commonweal*, June 1, 1996, p. 16.

Glossary

active euthanasia: Taking a deliberate action, such as injecting a lethal drug, to end a person's life for the purpose of relieving suffering. Compare to passive euthanasia.

advance directive: One of several types of legal document that competent adults may use to state their wishes about health care decisions to be made on their behalf if they become incompetent.

Alzheimer's disease: An incurable disease that causes slow destruction of the brain, with loss of memory and mental functions. It usually strikes the elderly.

assisted death: Any form of hastening a person's death, at his or her request, for the purpose of ending suffering, including physician-assisted suicide, euthanasia (in its narrower meaning), and, possibly, ending of life-sustaining medical treatment. Same as euthanasia in its broader meaning.

autonomy: Self-determination or independence; the right to control and make decisions about one's own life.

battery: The crime of touching someone without the person's permission, unless such touching is specifically permitted by law. Medical treatment given against someone's will is legally a form of battery.

brain stem: The base of the brain, located at the back of the neck. It controls automatic responses such as breathing and heartbeat. It usually continues to function in people who are in a persistent vegetative state.

chronic illness: An illness that lasts a long time or permanently.

coma: A state of deep and often permanent lack of awareness of one's environment; popular name for persistent vegetative state.

competent: Able to understand a complex subject such as health care and to make and communicate rational decisions about it.

controlled substances: Drugs that are often abused, such as narcotics. Their availability is therefore limited by special laws such as the Controlled Substances Act.

Death with Dignity Act: A law in Oregon that legalizes physician-assisted suicide for terminally ill people under certain conditions. The law was passed by voters in November 1994, but court challenges prevented it from going into effect until October 1997.

depression: A mental illness marked by powerful feelings of hopelessness and an inability to enjoy life. It can often be treated successfully by drugs, counseling, or a combination of the two.

double effect: Refers to an action that has an intended good effect and also a bad effect that can be predicted but is not desired. An example is a physician's giving a terminally ill person in pain a high dose of narcotics for the intended purpose of controlling the pain, knowing that the drugs may have the second, unintended effect of shortening or even ending the person's life. This action is also called terminal sedation.

due process clause: The part of the Fourteenth Amendment to the U.S. Constitution that reads, "No State shall deprive any person of life, liberty, or property without due process of law." The Supreme Court has ruled that this clause protects the liberty to make certain personal decisions, including those involved in marriage, bearing and raising children, and refusing medical treatment.

durable power of attorney for health care: A legal document in which competent adults appoint another person (a surrogate) to make health care decisions for them if they should become incompetent. It is also known as a health care proxy and is one form of an advance directive.

equal protection clause: The part of the Fourteenth Amendment to the U.S. Constitution that reads, "No State shall deny to any person within its jurisdiction the equal protection of the laws." The Supreme Court has interpreted this clause to mean that laws must treat similar groups in the same way.

ethics committee: A group made up of physicians, lawyers, ethicists, social workers, clergy, and others that helps health care professionals make difficult decisions involving medical ethics, such as whether to continue life-sustaining treatment for particular patients. Most hospitals have such committees.

euthanasia: Ending a person's life in order to relieve suffering. *Euthanasia* sometimes refers to any method of hastening a suffering person's death, including ending life-sustaining medical treatment, assisting in suicide, and taking direct action (such as giving a lethal injection) to cause death. At other times, it refers only to taking direct action to cause another's death.

Hippocratic oath: An oath supposed to have been written by the Greek physician Hippocrates, who lived during the fourth century B.C. It is still considered a major statement of medical ethics, and physicians often recite it when graduating from medical school. It includes a promise to "give no deadly drug, even when asked for it."

hospice: An institution or program that offers physical, psychological, and spiritual comfort to dying people and their families.

incompetent: Unable to make decisions about subjects such as health care because of being unconscious or suffering other severe lack of mental function. Compare to competent.

informed consent: Consent to receive a medical treatment after being told about the treatment's risks, benefits, and alternatives.

involuntary euthanasia: Killing a person for the purpose of relieving suffering without first obtaining the person's permission.

Lethal Drug Abuse Prevention Act: A proposed law that would have amended the Controlled Substances Act to require federal prosecution of doctors who prescribe a controlled substance knowing that it will be used for suicide. The act was introduced into Congress in July 1997 but withdrawn in October 1998 after medical and hospice groups criticized it. Its sponsors revised it and reintroduced it as the Pain Relief Promotion Act.

living will: A legal document in which a competent adult specifies medical treatments to be given or withheld if he or she becomes incompetent. It may also describe conditions under which the person wants all treatment stopped. A living will is one form of advance directive.

Pain Relief Promotion Act: Revised version of the Lethal Drug Abuse Prevention Act. The new act made a clearer distinction between use of controlled substances for pain relief and for assistance in suicide. It also added funding for a program to improve palliative care. The Pain Relief Promotion Act was introduced into Congress in June 1999, and the House of Representatives passed it in October.

palliative care: Care that gives comfort to dying or incurably ill people and their families but does not attempt to cure disease. It usually includes psychological and spiritual counseling as well as relief of unpleasant physical effects such as pain and nausea.

passive euthanasia: Refraining from or stopping an action, such as life-sustaining medical treatment, in order to let a terminally ill person die naturally.

pathologist: A physician who examines dead bodies or material removed from living people for signs of disease or injury.

Patient Self-Determination Act: An act passed by Congress in November 1990 that requires all health care institutions receiving federal funding to inform patients about their rights to fill out advance directives and refuse medical treatment.

persistent vegetative state: A deep and usually permanent state of unawareness, caused by damage to the higher brain. People in this state may make automatic responses such as breathing, heartbeat, and random movements and sounds, but they are not conscious of their surroundings. A persistent vegetative state is popularly called a coma.

physician-assisted suicide: An act in which a physician provides the means for suicide, usually a prescription for a lethal dose of drugs, to someone who is terminally or incurably ill. The patient must take the final action that causes his or her death, such as swallowing the drugs.

Remmelink Report: An influential report issued by the government of the Netherlands in 1991 to provide statistics about the practice of physician-assisted suicide and euthanasia in that country. It was updated by a second report in 1995.

respirator: A device that forces air into and out of the lungs of a person who cannot breathe naturally.

Rights of the Terminally Ill Act: A law that was effective in Australia's Northern Territory between July 1996 and March 1997, when the Australian Parliament repealed it. The law allowed terminally ill people to receive a doctor's assistance in suicide under certain conditions.

right-to-die movement: A social and political movement to guarantee the legal right to have some degree of control over the time and manner of one's death, which may include the right to request a physician's aid in dying.

right-to-life movement: A social and political movement based on the religious belief that human life should be preserved under all circumstances. The movement strongly opposes abortion and all forms of assisted dying.

slippery slope argument: Argument based on the idea that certain acts, although not morally wrong in themselves, unavoidably lead to other acts that are wrong. For right-to-die opponents, this argument means that social or legal acceptance of each stage of aid in dying (refusal of life-sustaining treatment, physician-assisted suicide, voluntary euthanasia) is bound to lead to the next stage, eventually resulting in euthanasia committed against a person's will. The argument can also refer to broadening of the categories of people who are eligible for aid in dying, beginning with terminally ill, competent adults and ending with competent elderly or disabled people who have not given their consent.

surrogate: A person appointed to make decisions, including health care decisions, on behalf of an incompetent person. Competent adults may choose surrogates in advance by filling out durable powers of attorney for health care. Courts may appoint surrogates for people who have never been competent or have not previously chosen a surrogate for themselves.

terminal illness: An illness expected to cause death in a short time, usually within six months.

voluntary euthanasia: Killing a person at the person's request for the purpose of relieving the person's suffering from a terminal or incurable illness or injury.

Organizations
to Contact

American Civil Liberties Union (ACLU)
125 Broad St.
New York, NY 10004-2400
(212) 549-2585
e-mail: aclu@aclu.org
website: www.aclu.org

This large civil rights organization supports people's right to make choices about their lives and has supported challenges to laws against assisted suicide. The ACLU publishes press releases, news updates, and a newsletter on issues related to civil liberties.

American Foundation for Suicide Prevention
120 Wall St., 22nd Fl.
New York, NY 10005
(888) 333-2377
e-mail: inquiry@afsp.org
website: www.afsp.org

This group, headed by psychiatrist Herbert Hendin, supports research and education on depression and suicide. It opposes legalization of physician-assisted suicide. Its website offers a position paper and other materials giving reasons for opposing physician-assisted suicide.

American Life League
PO Box 1350
Stafford, VA 22555
(540) 659-4171
e-mail: jbrown@all.org
website: www.all.org

This group believes that all human life is sacred and opposes legalization of euthanasia. It distributes newsletters, videos, and brochures about developments related to euthanasia and other pro-life issues.

American Medical Association (AMA)
515 N. State St.
Chicago, IL 60610
(312) 464-5000
website: www.ama-assn.org

The American Medical Association is the chief physicians' association in the United States. It opposes physician-assisted suicide and euthanasia and supports improvements in palliative care.

Americans for Better Care of the Dying
2175 K St. NW, Suite 820
Washington, DC 20037
(202) 530-9864
e-mail: caring@erols.com
website: www.abcd-caring.com

This group is dedicated to social, professional, and policy reform that will improve the care system for patients with serious or terminal illnesses. It also sponsors public and professional education about end-of-life care and publishes educational materials and a newsletter.

American Society of Law, Medicine, and Ethics
765 Commonwealth Ave., 16th Fl.
Boston, MA 02215
(617) 262-4990
e-mail: info@aslme.org
website: www.aslme.org

This group acts as a forum for discussion of issues including euthanasia and physician-assisted suicide. It publishes quarterly journals, a newsletter, and books. It also has an information clearinghouse and a library.

Association for Death Education and Counseling
342 N. Main Street
West Hartford, CT 06117-2507
e-mail: info@adec.org
(860) 586-7503
website: www.adec.org

This association is dedicated to improving the quality of death education and death-related counseling and caregiving.

Center for the Rights of the Terminally Ill
PO Box 54246
Hurst, TX 76054-2064
(817) 656-5143

The center opposes assisted suicide and euthanasia and works to protect the disabled, the elderly, the sick, and the dying from the threats presented by these practices.

Choice in Dying (CID)
1035 30· St. NW
Washington, DC 20007
(800) 989-9455
e-mail: cid@choices.org
website: www.choices.org

CID is dedicated to improving communication among patients, families, and health care professionals about end-of-life decisions. It distributes advance directives, booklets about end-of-life decisions, and a newsletter. It is in the process of forming a new group called Partnership for Caring.

Citizens United Resisting Euthanasia (CURE)
812 Stephen St.
Berkeley Springs, WV 25411
(304) 258-5433
e-mail: cureltd@ix.netcom.com
website: pweb.netcom.com/~cureltd/index.html

CURE strongly opposes all forms of euthanasia and defends the right of patients to receive life-sustaining medical treatments. Its website contains a variety of educational brochures and position papers as well as newspaper and magazine articles supporting its point of view.

Compassionate Healthcare Network

PO Box 62548
12874 96th Ave.
Surrey, BC V3V 7V6, Canada

The network opposes euthanasia and physician-assisted suicide and favors advance directives and improvements in palliative care. It provides speakers, videos, and workshops as well as research data pertaining to euthanasia, assisted suicide, palliative care, and advance directives.

Compassion in Dying

6312 SW Capitol Hwy., Suite 415
Portland, OR 97201
(503) 221-9556
e-mail: info@CompassionInDying.org
website: www.CompassionInDying.org

This group provides client service, legal advocacy, and public education to improve management of pain and other physical problems, increase patient self-determination, and expand end-of-life choices to include aid in dying for terminally ill, mentally competent adults. It publishes a quarterly newsletter.

Death with Dignity National Center

1818 N Street, NW, Suite 450
Washington, DC 20036
(202) 530-2900
e-mail: admin@deathwithdignity.org
website: www.deathwithdignity.org

This group promotes a comprehensive, humane system of care for terminally ill patients and works to increase such patients' choices and autonomy. It acts as an information resource on right-to-die issues.

Dying Well Network
PO Box 880
Spokane, WA 99210-0880
(509) 926-2457
e-mail: Rob.Neils@ior.com
website: www.ior.com/~jeffw/homepage.htm

The network supports the right of a competent, terminally ill adult to choose the time and manner of his or her death, within the law. Volunteers supply information to terminally ill people and their families.

Dying with Dignity
55 Eglinton Ave. East, Suite 705
Toronto, ON M4P 1G8, Canada
(800) 495-6156
e-mail: dwdca@web.net
website: www.web.net/dwd/

This Canadian society is concerned with the quality of dying. It advises patients about their right to choose health care options at the end of life, distributes advance directives, and works for legal changes to support advance directives and permit voluntary, physician-assisted dying. The group publishes a newsletter.

Euthanasia Prevention Coalition BC
103-2609 Westview Dr., Suite 126
North Vancouver, BC V7N 4N2, Canada
(604) 794-3772
e-mail: info@epc.bc.ca
website: www.epc.bc.ca

This group opposes legalization or promotion of euthanasia and physician-assisted suicide. It educates the public about the risks of these activities and advises on alternative methods of relieving suffering.

Euthanasia Research and Guidance Organization (ERGO)
24829 Norris Ln.
Junction City, OR 97448-9559
(541) 998-1873
e-mail: ergo@efn.org
website: www.finalexit.org/

ERGO supports choice and, if necessary, help in dying for those who desire it. It advises terminally ill people and their families about euthanasia through literature and on-line material; its website has extensive resources.

Growth House, Inc.

San Francisco, CA
(415) 255-9045
e-mail: info@growthhouse.org
website: www.growthhouse.org/

Growth House works to improve the quality of compassionate (palliative) care for the dying as an alternative to assisted suicide and euthanasia. Its website provides resources for end-of-life care.

Hastings Center

Garrison, NY 10524
(914) 424-4040
website: www.thehastingscenter.org/

The center addresses fundamental ethical issues in health, medicine, and the environment, including euthanasia and physician-assisted suicide. It publishes a bimonthly journal, the *Hastings Center Report*, and other papers.

Hemlock Society

PO Box 101810
Denver, CO 80250-1810
(800) 247-7421
e-mail: hemlock@privatei.com
website: www.hemlock.org/hemlock

This is the oldest, largest, and best-known right-to-die organization in the United States. It works for increased choice in dying, including legalization of physician-assisted suicide, through lobbying, education, and patient advocacy. It provides educational material through its website; a quarterly newsletter, *TimeLines;* and brochures.

Human Life International
4 Family Life Ln.
Front Royal, VA 22630
(540) 635-7884
e-mail: hli@hli.org
website: www.hli.org

This group believes that euthanasia and assisted suicide are morally unacceptable. It publishes monthly newsletters and on-line articles on euthanasia.

International Anti-Euthanasia Task Force
PO Box 760
Steubenville, OH 43952
(740) 282-3810
E-mail: info@iaetf.org
website: http://iaetf.org

This organization opposes all forms of euthanasia and tries to influence the public, legislators, and the courts to ban them. It supplies an on-line library of resources.

Last Acts Coalition
c/o Ms. Nancy Reller
Barksdale Ballard & Co.
1951 Kidwell Dr., Suite 205
Vienna, VA 22182
(703) 827-8771
e-mail: nreller@bballard.com
website: www.lastacts.org

This coalition of health care organizations and others works to improve care of the dying as an alternative to physician-assisted suicide. It helps to arrange for speakers and other resources.

National Right to Life Committee
419 Seventh St. NW, Suite 500
Washington, DC 20004
(202) 626-8800
e-mail: nrlc@nrlc.org
website: www.nrlc.org

This organization opposes physician-assisted suicide and euthanasia. Its publications include a monthly newsletter and a
position paper explaining its reasons for opposing the legalization of assisted suicide.

Not Dead Yet
c/o Diane Coleman
7521 Madison St.
Forest Park, IL 60130
(708) 209-1500
website: www.notdeadyet.org

This national grassroots disability rights organization opposes legalization of physician-assisted suicide and euthanasia because of risks it believes such actions present to
disabled and chronically ill people.

**Oregon Death with Dignity Legal Defense and Education
Center**
818 S.W. Third Ave., Suite 218
Portland, OR 97204
(503) 228-6079
e-mail: info@dwd.org
website: www.dwd.org

This group provides information, education, research, and
support for a comprehensive range of end-of-life options, including physician-assisted suicide under certain conditions.
It works to defend and educate people about Oregon's Death
with Dignity Act.

Project on Death in America
Open Society Institute
400 W. 59th St.
New York, NY 10019
e-mail: pdia@sorosny.org
website: www.soros.org/death/index.htm

The project works to understand and transform the culture
and experience of dying and bereavement through initiatives

in research, scholarship, the humanities, and the arts. It fosters innovations in the provision of care, public and professional education, and public policy.

World Federation of Right to Die Societies
c/o ERGO
24829 Norris Ln.
Junction City, OR 97448-9559
(541) 998-3285
e-mail: mikelib@bigpond.com
website: www.finalexit.org/world.fed.html

This international federation supports the right of the terminally ill to choose the time and manner of their death and to ask for assistance in dying if necessary. It publishes a newsletter and reports of conferences.

Suggestions for Further Reading

Books

Laura K. Egendorf, ed., *Current Controversies: Assisted Suicide*. San Diego: Greenhaven, 1998. This anthology provides pro and con essays on whether assisted suicide is ethical, whether it is a constitutional right, whether it should be legalized, and whether it would threaten individuals' rights.

Peter G. Filene, *In the Arms of Others: A Cultural History of the Right-to-Die in America*. Chicago: Ivan R. Dee, 1998. Provides an interesting, readable history of the right-to-die movement, with a focus on the Karen Quinlan case.

Derek Humphry and Mary Clement, *Freedom to Die: People, Politics, and the Right-to-Die Movement*. New York: St. Martin's, 1998. An extensive history of the right-to-die movement by one of its founders.

Derek Humphrey and Ann Wickett, *The Right to Die: An Historical and Legal Perspective of Euthanasia*. Eugene, OR: Hemlock Society, 1990. Describes the early history of the right-to-die movement (1970s and 1980s) and provides historical background on attitudes toward suicide, early attempts to legalize euthanasia, the Nazi "euthanasia" program, and other factors that have shaped modern attitudes toward euthanasia.

Edward J. Larson and Darrel W. Amundsen, *A Different Death: Euthanasia and the Christian Tradition*. Downers Grove, IL: InterVarsity, 1998. Describes Christian attitudes toward euthanasia from early Christianity to the present day.

James D. Torr, ed., *Opposing Viewpoints Digests: Euthanasia*. San Diego: Greenhaven, 1999. Summarizes pro and con positions on whether euthanasia is ethical, whether physicians should participate in euthanasia, and whether voluntary euthanasia should be legalized.

James D. Torr, ed., *Opposing Viewpoints: Euthanasia*. San Diego: Greenhaven, 2000. An anthology of pro and con essays that considers whether euthanasia is ethical, whether voluntary euthanasia should be legalized, whether legalizing euthanasia would lead to involuntary killing, and whether physicians should assist in suicide.

Sue Woodman, *Last Rights: The Struggle over the Right to Die*. New York: Plenum, 1998. This easy-to-read history of the right-to-die movement provides background on the movement's leaders, the kind of people who join it, reactions to it, and example cases that illustrate the difficult decisions involved.

Periodicals

Marcia Angell, "The Supreme Court and Physician-Assisted Suicide—the Ultimate Right," *New England Journal of Medicine*, January 2, 1997.

Tom Duffy, "In the Name of Mercy: The Anti-Kevorkian Dr. Timothy Quill Makes His Case for Assisted Suicide," *People Weekly*, April 7, 1997.

Ezekiel Emanuel, "Whose Right to Die?" *Atlantic Monthly*, March 1997.

Linda L. Emanuel, "Facing Requests for Physician-Assisted Suicide," *Journal of the American Medical Association*, August 19, 1998.

Lawrence O. Gostin, "Deciding Life and Death in the Courtroom," *Journal of the American Medical Association*, November 12, 1997.

Ernest van den Haag, "Make Mine Hemlock," *National Review*, June 12, 1995.

Steve Hallock, "Physician-Assisted Suicide: 'Slippery Slope' or Civil Right?" *Humanist*, July-August 1996.

Herbert Hendin, Chris Rutenfrans and Zbigniew Zylicz, "Physician-Assisted Suicide and Euthanasia in the Netherlands: Lessons from the Dutch," *Journal of the American Medical Association*, June 4, 1997.

Jack Kevorkian, "A Modern Inquisition," *Utne Reader*, March-April 1995.

Thomas A. Shannon, "Physician-Assisted Suicide: Ten Questions," *Commonweal*, June 1, 1996.

William Swanson, "Mortal Concern," *Minneapolis–St. Paul Magazine*, October 1996.

Gary L. Thomas, "Deadly Compassion," *Christianity Today*, June 16, 1997.

Paul Wilkes, "The Next Pro-Lifers," *New York Times Magazine*, July 21, 1996.

Websites

Death Education
(www.fidnet.com/~weid/deathed.htm#top). This site has links to information about death, grief, hospice, and many related topics. It has a subsite devoted to euthanasia and assisted suicide at www.fidnet.com/~weid/deathed. htm#euthanasia. This includes a glossary of terms, a frequently-asked-questions (FAQ) sheet about death with dignity, and a fact sheet about euthanasia in the Netherlands.

Deathnet (www.rights.org/deathnet/open.html). Includes news bulletins, an extensive list of books about topics related to death and dying, an even more extensive on-line library, advance directives and other legal documents, links to a variety of sites related to death and health care, and laws and court cases related to the right-to-die movement.

Ethics Update Euthanasia Site (http://ethics.acusd.edu/
euthanasia.html). This site on euthanasia and end-of-life
decisions includes discussion forums and questions, Internet
resources, a bibliography, legal decisions, and web links.

Sociology of Death and Dying (www.trinity.edu/~mkearl/
death.html). This site, established by Professor Michael
Kearl of Trinity University in San Antonio, Texas, covers
not only euthanasia and related right-to-die issues but also
such topics as death across cultures and time, death in the
arts, "immortality capitalism style," experiences of being in
contact with the dead, death-related urban legends, and
personal impacts of death.

Yahoo! Assisted Suicide Site (http://headlines.yahoo.com/
Full_Coverage/US/Assisted_Suicide). This site includes
current newspaper articles and links to other websites and
chat rooms related to assisted suicide.

Works Consulted

Books

Maureen Harrison and Steve Gilbert, eds., *Life, Death, and the Law.* San Diego: Excellent Books, 1997. Provides edited text of court decisions in the cases of Karen Quinlan, Nancy Cruzan, and the Washington and New York right-to-die cases reviewed by the Supreme Court in 1997.

Albert R. Jonsen, Robert M. Veatch, and LeRoy Walters, eds., *Source Book in Bioethics: A Documentary History.* Washington, DC: Georgetown University Press, 1998. This book contains a section on the ethics of death and dying, including abridged text of the Karen Quinlan and Nancy Cruzan court decisions.

John Keown, ed., *Euthanasia Examined: Ethical, Clinical, and Legal Perspectives.* Cambridge, England: Cambridge University Press, 1995. This collection of eighteen essays provides pro and con discussions on such subjects as the ethics of euthanasia, whether patients in persistent vegetative states should be fed, legal and theological aspects of euthanasia, and euthanasia in the Netherlands.

Gregory E. Pence, *Classic Cases in Medical Ethics.* New York: McGraw-Hill, 1995. Contains a section on cases about death and dying, providing background and analysis of legal and ethical aspects of each. Includes cases involving people in comas, disabled people's requests for assistance in suicide, and ethical questions raised by the activities of Jack Kevorkian.

Michael M. Uhlmann, ed., *Last Rights: Assisted Suicide and Euthanasia Debated.* Grand Rapids, MI: William B. Eerdmans, 1998. This anthology of essays discusses classical, Christian, and early modern thought on suicide and contemporary moral, theological, medical, and legal perspectives on assisted suicide and euthanasia.

Periodicals

Ann Alpers and Bernard Lo, "Does It Make Clinical Sense to Equate Terminally Ill Patients Who Require Life-Sustaining Interventions with Those Who Do Not?" *Journal of the American Medical Association*, June 4, 1997.

Associated Press, "Fifteen Assisted Suicides Under New Oregon Law," *San Francisco Chronicle*, February 18, 1999.

Anthony L. Back et al., "Physician-Assisted Suicide and Euthanasia in Washington State," *Journal of the American Medical Association*, March 27, 1996.

Katie Baer, "The Final Chapter," *Harvard Health Letter*, February 1995.

John M. Benson, "The Polls—Trends in End-of-Life Issues," *Public Opinion Quarterly*, Summer 1999.

Peter J. Bernardi, "The Hidden Engines of the Suicide Rights Movement," *America*, May 6, 1995.

Michael Betzold, "The Selling of Doctor Death: How Jack Kevorkian Became a National Hero," *New Republic*, May 26, 1997.

Christian Century, "Foes of Assisted Suicide Marshal Arguments," *Lancet*, March 19, 1997.

John L. Collins and Frank T. Brennan, "Euthanasia and the Potential Adverse Effects for Northern Territory Aborigines," *Lancet*, June 28, 1997.

Jessica Cooper, "Consider Yourself Stopped," *National Right to Life News*, May 11, 1999.

Paul Cotton, "Medicine's Position Is Both Pivotal and Precarious in Assisted-Suicide Debate," *Journal of the American Medical Association*, February 1, 1995.

"Curtains for Dr. Death," *Time*, April 5, 1999.

Ezekiel J. Emanuel, "The End of Euthanasia? Death's Door," *New Republic*, May 17, 1999.

Ezekiel J. and Linda L. Emanuel, "The Promise of a Good Death," *Lancet*, May 16, 1998.

Ezekiel J. Emanuel et al., "The Practice of Euthanasia and Physician-Assisted Suicide in the United States," *Journal of the American Medical Association*, August 12, 1998.

Jerry Filteau, "Suicide Ruling Spurs Wide Opposition," *National Catholic Reporter*, March 22, 1996.

Michael Fumento, "Euthanasia in Netherlands Is Cautionary Tale for U.S.," *Insight on the News*, April 17, 1995.

Robert P. George and William C. Porth Jr., "Death, Be Not Proud," *National Review*, June 26, 1995.

David Heim, "Being Creatures," *Christian Century*, July 17-24, 1996.

Leon R. Kass and Nelson Lund, "Courting Death: Assisted Suicide, Doctors, and the Law," *Commentary*, December 1996.

David W. Kissane, Annette Street, and Philip Nitschke, "Seven Deaths in Darwin," *Lancet*, October 3, 1998.

Art Levine, "In Oregon, a Political Campaign to Die For: Assisted Suicide Fight Turns Ugly," *U.S. News & World Report*, November 10, 1997.

Paul J. van der Maas et al., "Euthanasia, Physician-Assisted Suicide, and Other Medical Practices Involving the End of Life in the Netherlands, 1990–1995," *New England Journal of Medicine*, November 28, 1996.

Richard A. McCormick, "Viva la Difference! Killing and Allowing to Die," *America*, December 6, 1997.

Paul R. McHugh, "The Kevorkian Epidemic," *American Scholar*, Winter 1997.

New York Task Force on Life and the Law, "The Risks of

Legalization," *National Right to Life News*, March 11, 1998.

Randall E. Otto, "Bottom of the Slope," *Commonweal*, May 19, 1995.

Pope John Paul II, "Excerpts from *Evangelium Vitae*," *National Catholic Reporter*, April 7, 1995.

Sara Rimer, "Focus on Seniors' Depression," *New York Times*, reprinted in *San Francisco Chronicle*, September 5, 1999.

Joseph P. Shapiro, "Euthanasia's Home: What the Dutch Experience Can Teach Americans About Assisted Suicide," *U.S. News & World Report*, January 13, 1997.

Joseph P. Shapiro with David Bowermaster, "Death on Trial," *U.S. News & World Report*, April 25, 1994.

Wesley J. Smith, "Assisted Suicide Isn't 'Death with Dignity,'" *San Francisco Chronicle*, November 12, 1998.

"Terminal Care: Too Painful, Too Prolonged," *Newsweek,* December 4, 1995.

Michael Walzer, "Feed the Face," *New Republic*, June 9, 1997.

Kathi Wolfe, "Disabled Activists Fight Assisted Suicide," *Progressive*, September 1996.

Index

active euthanasia, 23
Adkins, Janet, 26–27
advance directives, 18–19, 42–43
AIDS, 24
Alexander, Leo, 71–72
Alzheimer's disease, 27
American Euthanasia Society, 50
American Foundation for Suicide Prevention, 62
American Medical Association (AMA), 26, 32, 33
American Nurses Association, 33
Andrews, Kevin, 58
Angell, Marcia, 34, 36
assisted death
  forms of, 8–9
  growing support for, 23–24
  Humphry's views on, 21–23
  See also physician-assisted suicide; suicide, assisted
Australia, euthanasia in, 57–59
autonomy, 69–70

battery, 41
Baulche, Burke, 68
Borst-Eilers, Else, 33

Bosscher, Hilly, 64, 65
brain damage, 19

California legislation, 51
cancer, 10
Caplan, Arthur, 66
Catholic Church, 32, 47, 51
Center for the Rights of the Terminally Ill, 91
Chabot, Boudewijn, 64
children
  refusal of care for, 44
Christian Century (Heim), 9
Christianity, 45
chronic care, 36–37
Citizens United Resisting Euthanasia (CURE), 91
civil rights movement, 13–14
Cohen, Herbert, 66
Coleman, Diane, 49, 73
comas, 15, 19
comfort care, 34–36
Compassion in Dying, 44
Compassion in Dying et al. v. State of Washington, 46–47
competence, 57
Concern for Dying, 23
consciousness, 15, 19
consent, informed, 41

Constantine, Thomas, 53
controlled substances, 53–54
Cooper, Jessica (judge), 30
Courts
  of Appeals, Ninth Circuit,
    46, 53
  of Appeals, Second Circuit,
    48
Cruzan, Joe and Joyce, 19
Cruzan case, 18–21, 42

death
  natural, 6–7
  society's attitudes toward,
    14–15
  statistics on, 13, 61–62, 63
Death with Dignity Act,
  51–53, 55
Dent, Bob, 59
depression, 29, 36, 64–66
dignity, fear of losing, 10,
  56, 70
disabled people, threats to,
  66, 72–73
doctor-assisted death. See
  physician-assisted suicide
Doctor Death. See Kevorkian,
  Jack
doctors
  better education, on dying,
    38–39
  role of, 26, 32–33
  terminal sedation and, 31–32
Dority, Barbara, 10
double effect, 31–32
due process clause, 45–46, 47
Dutch medical guidelines,
  59–60, 65–66

Dutch Supreme Court,
  64–65
dying process, prolonging,
  12–13

education, 38–39
Emanuel, Ezekiel J., 57, 68
end-of-life care, 34–36,
  38–39
equal protection clause,
  45–46, 48, 52
euthanasia
  active, 23
  advocates for, 75–76
  critics of, 57, 62–64, 75, 77
  debates over, 28–30, 68–69,
    77
  doctor's role in, 26
  ethical principles in, 8–9
  idea of, 10–12
  legalization of
    support for and against,
      32–34, 50–53
  meaning of, 6–8
  for mental distress, 29, 36,
    64–66
  passive, type, 21
  see also legislation;
    physician-assisted suicide
Euthanasia Education
  Council, 18
Euthanasia Laws Bill, 58
Euthanasia Society of
  America, 11

feeding tubes, removal of,
  13, 20–21
Fenigsen, Richard, 64

Fieger, Geoffrey, 29
food and water
  refusal of, 19–20
Fourteenth Amendment
  violations under the, 45,
    46, 47, 53

George, Robert P., 75
Gilman, Charlotte Perkins, 70
*Glucksberg v. Washington
  State*, 46, 49–50
Gostin, Lawrence O., 40
Griesa, Thomas (judge), 48
Grossman, Howard, 32

health care
  durable power of attorney
    for, 18, 21
  proxy, 18
  rising cost of, 36–37, 74
Heim, David, 9
Hemlock Society, 10, 22, 51
Hendin, Herbert, 62–64
Heston, Delores, 42
Hippocratic oath, 25
Hogan, Michael (judge), 52
hospice care, 35–36
hospital deaths, 13
How We Die (Nuland), 13
Humphry, Derek, 21–23, 29
Hyde, Henry, 53

incurable illnesses, 10–11,
  27
independence, 56, 69–70
informed consent, 41
Jean's Way (Humphry), 21–22
John Paul II (pope), 72

Joondeph, Bob, 72

Katz, Ira, 36
Keene, Barry, 18
Kevorkian, Jack
  criticism against, 28–29
  murder trial of, 29–30
  patients of, 26–28
Kübler-Ross, Elisabeth, 15

*Last Rights: Struggle over
  the Right to Die, The*
  (Woodman), 28
laws. *See* legislation
Lee, Barbara Coombs, 56
legislation
  on advance directives,
    17–18
  against assisted suicide,
    44–46
  campaigns for new, 50–51
  Controlled Substances Act,
    53
  Death with Dignity Act,
    51–53, 55
  on duty to preserve life,
    41–42
  Lethal Drug Abuse
    Prevention Act, 53–54
  Pain Relief Promotion Act,
    54
  Patient Self-Determination
    Act, 43
  on right to refuse treatment,
    40–41
  see also specific states
lethal prescriptions, 21, 24,
  46, 51, 55

Let Me Die Before I Wake
  (Humphry), 22–23
Levinson, Ann Jane, 23
life passports, 66
life prolongation
  decisions concerning,
    41–42
  treatment promoting,
    12–13
life-sustaining treatment
  debates over, 16, 18–21,
    41–42
living wills, 17–18
Longmore, Paul, 73
long-term care, 36–37
Lynn, Joanne, 74

medical advances, 6, 12–13
Medicare, 37, 74
medication, lethal doses, 21,
  24, 46, 51, 55
mental distress
  euthanasia for, 64–66
Mercitron, 26, 27
mercy killing, 7
Michigan legislation, 29
Miner, Roger (judge), 34, 48
Missouri Supreme Court
  decision, 20–21, 42
Morse, Robert, 15, 26
Muir, Robert, Jr., 16

National Right to Life
  Committee, 68
natural death, 6–7, 16
Natural Death Act, 18
Nazi "euthanasia" program,
  11–12

Netherlands, the
  differences between United
    States and, 66–67
  euthanasia in, 59–60,
    64–66
  Remmelink Report, 61–62
  slippery slope argument,
    62–64
*New England Journal of
  Medicine*, 30
New Jersey Supreme Court
  decision, 16, 42
New York
  legislation in, 44, 50
New York State v. Quill, 44,
  47–48, 49–50
New York Task Force on
  Life, 74
Nickles, Don, 53
Nitschke, Philip, 58–59
Noonan, John T., Jr. (judge),
  46–47
Not Dead Yet, 49, 73
Nuland, Sherwin, 13

Ohio
  legislation in, 50
On Death and Dying
  (Kübler-Ross), 15
Oregon
  Death with Dignity Act,
    51–53
  experience with euthanasia,
    55–57
Oregon Advocacy Center, 72

Pain Relief Promotion Act,
  54

palliative care, 34–36, 38–39
passive euthanasia, 21
Patient Self-Determination
  Act, 43
patients' rights movement,
  14
patients' wishes,
  determining, 20, 42–44
  see also advance directives
Pellegrino, Edmund, 60, 63
Perron, Marshall, 57
persistent vegetative state
  (PVS), 15, 26
physician-assisted suicide
  Australia's report on,
    57–59
  debates over, 28–30,
    68–69, 77
  definition of, 7–8
  Dr. Kevorkian and, 26–28
  Dr. Quill and, 30–31
  Dutch guidelines on, 59–60
  ethical principles in, 8–9,
    69–70
  legalization of
    support for and against,
      32–34, 50–53
  Oregon's report on, 55–57
  Remmelink Report, 61–62
physicians
  better education, on dying,
    38–39
  duties of, 26, 32–33
terminal sedation and, 31–32
*Planned Parenthood of
  Southeastern Pennsylvania
  v. Casey*, 47
Porth, William C., Jr., 75

Postma, Geertruida, 60
power of attorney, durable,
  18, 21
preservation of life
  state interests in, 16, 41–42
Publishers Weekly, 15

Quill, Timothy, 30–31
*Quill v. New York Attorney
  General*, 48, 49–50
Quill v. Vacco, 48
Quinlan, Joseph, 15–16
Quinlan, Julia, 15, 19
Quinlan, Karen Ann, 15–17
Quinlan case ruling, 42

Reardon, Thomas, 33
refusal of treatment
  debate over, 16, 18–21,
    40–41
Rehnquist, William (Chief
  Justice), 20, 49–50, 54
Reinhardt, Stephen (judge),
  9, 47
religious views, 9, 42, 45, 47
Remmelink Report, 61–62
Reno, Janet, 53
respirators, disconnecting,
  13, 16, 26
Rights of the Terminally Ill
  Act, 57–59
right to choose to die
  Cruzan case and, 18–21
  ethics and legality of,
    28–29, 44–46, 69–70
  New York case and, 47–48
  Quinlan case and, 15–17
  U.S. Supreme Court ruling,

49–50, 54
Washington case and,
   46–47
right-to-die movement, 10,
   24, 28
right to refuse treatment
   debates over, 16, 18–21,
   40–41
Roe v. Wade, 47
Rothstein, Barbara (judge), 46
Royal Dutch Medical
   Association, 60
Rudin, A. James (rabbi), 72
Russell, Bertrand, 11

Saunders, Dame Cicely, 35
self-determination, 69–70
Shaw, George Bernard, 11
St. Christopher's (hospice), 35
suicide, assisted
   critics of, 57, 62–64
   growing support for, 23–24
   Humphry's views on,
      21–23, 28–29
   legalization of
      support for and against,
         32–34, 50–53

legislation on, 44–46
see also physician-assisted
   suicide
surrogates, 21, 42

terminally ill patients
   definition of, 7
   rights of, 21, 28, 44–46, 71
terminal sedation, 32, 61
Thomas, Gary L., 24

Vacco, Dennis, 74
voluntary euthanasia, 61, 62,
   63
Voluntary Euthanasia
   Society, 11

Washington State legislation,
   44, 51
*Washington State v.
   Glucksberg*, 46, 49–50
Wells, H. G., 11
Wickett, Ann, 22
wills, living, 17–18
World Health Organization,
   35

Picture Credits

About the Author

Lisa Yount earned a bachelor's degree with honors in English and creative writing from Stanford University. She has a lifelong interest in medicine and biology. She has been a professional writer for more than thirty years, producing educational materials, magazine articles, and some thirty books for young people and adults. Her books for Lucent include *Biomedical Ethics*, *Cancer*, and *Epidemics*. She lives in El Cerrito, California, with her husband, a large library, and several cats.